Traffic congestion goes through the issue-machine

A case-study in issue processing, illustrating a new approach

David Braybrooke

Professor of Political Science,
Dalhousie University, Nova Scotia

Routledge & Kegan Paul
London and Boston

First published 1974
by Routledge & Kegan Paul Ltd
Broadway House, 68–74 Carter Lane,
London EC4V 5EL
and 9 Park Street, Boston, Mass. 02108, U.S.A.
Printed in Great Britain by
W & J Mackay Limited, Chatham

ISBN 0 7100 7749 1

Library of Congress Catalog Card No 73–87314

To family and friends, present and departed, with whom I have cherished many things in England.

Contents

Fold-outs

Fold-out I

Definitions and abbreviations

Proposed policies a, b, c, d etc.

Properties of proposed policies C, N, S, E etc.

Cx= x is C
(Sometimes I shall use 'Cx' etc. to mean 'the property C that is ascribed to the proposed policy x')

S-stability: The same 'stations' appear in the issue-processing network during consecutive rounds and operate in the same sequence.

P-stability: The same issue-processing program (a tree of questions and instructions) is applied during consecutive rounds.

a= Extend and intensify parking controls beyond policies in force in 1963.

a′= Extend and intensify parking controls beyond policies in force in 1966.

b= Institute full road-pricing

c= Reconstruct cities so as to create a firm distinction between primary road-networks and protected environmental areas.

d= Build roads to an extent well beyond road construction already planned.

Let 'x' be a logical variable ranging over 'a,' 'a′,' 'b,' 'c,' 'd,' and possibly other proposals.

Cx=x would entail some check to the growth of traffic congestion.

Nx=x would bring net benefits not all of which can be expected from other policies in force or proposed.

Sx=x has a precedent technically successful and well-accepted by the public.

Ex=x would achieve an economic optimum of road-use (for motorists).

Ax=x would safeguard the amenities of town life.

Rx=x would bring about an increase, intolerable to motorists, of vexations from regulations.

Ix=x would interfere excessively with circulation and access for motorists.

Bx=x would impose an intolerable increase in the already excessive burden of taxation falling on motor-vehicle owners.

∼Wx= *x is *not* capable of being carried out (unworkable in that sense).

Kx=x requires expenditures far beyond those that can be budgeted in the foreseeable future.

Jx=x arouses vociferous opposition, which cannot for the time being be dissipated, from concerned groups outside Whitehall.

Lx=x is accepted without protest by the Greater London Council.

Sx ,,, Nx abbreviates the modus ponens argument [(Sx→Nx) & Sx, therefore Nx].

* Initially; but see secs. 5.2.1 and 5.2.2.

Preface

The aims of this little book, as indicated on the title page and as explained, briefly, but I hope tolerably fully, in Chapter 1 of the text proper, are twofold. I wish to try out—in several different versions—the idea that a political system, even when it does not process an issue entirely within one formal organization, in effect puts it through a standing 'machine,' used again and again for issues in a given field, and composed of a stable network of participating stations or (at least) manifested in a stable program of reasons pro and con—a program of a sort that could be run on a computer to simulate the operation of the political system in this connection. Trying out this idea is the chief aim of the book. In the course of achieving this I have been able, I think, to achieve another aim: The several versions given of the 'issue-machine' that may be supposed to have dealt with the issue of traffic congestion in the United Kingdom during the years 1963 to 1968 add up, taken together with the background narrative that I supply, to a substantial case-history. I have taken care not to sacrifice the inherent interest of this case-history to my methodological experiments. In fact the aim of giving an interesting case-history has seemed not to conflict in any serious way with what I have aimed at doing methodologically, even though, to make the points that I have wished most to make in pursuit of the methodological aim, I have had, in the central parts of my discussion, to introduce drastic simplifications both as to the number of proposals treated and as to the logical techniques used in describing the ways in which these proposals were processed. (The reasons for these simplifications and their significance are explained in Chapter 4 of the text.)

Almost every point of fact to be found in my text can be documented—as my notes will show—by published materials: White Papers, reports, pamphlets put out by HM Government or by the Greater London Council; books and pamphlets from private sources; the printed minutes of the GLC; reports in *The Times*. Obviously, documents of this sort do not tell the whole story of issue-processing on any subject; but one thing that this book may show is that they, in lieu of more detailed evidence about actions and reactions among the persons involved, can serve as the foundation for exhibiting the character and chief interconnections of the reasons that determine issue-processing in a given field of policy. The more detailed evidence is not available generally: political scientists cannot expect to sit in during all crucial deliberations, among officials and opinion leaders, let alone be present at all significant personal conversations; nor can they expect to recover commensurably much detailed information from interviews with participants, since the participants' memories are not sufficiently exact or comprehensive, and the participants cannot anyway spare the amount of interviewing time that would be required, were their memories superhuman.

During sojourns in London made possible by subventions from the Canada Council, I interviewed most, if not all, of the persons who took leading parts in discussions in the United Kingdom during the period 1963–8 on policy respecting traffic congestion; and what I was told during interviews has (I believe) helped me immeasurably by indicating to me what topics and materials to select and warning me away from false or confused interpretations. However, this much help, beyond the documents themselves, any investigator may hope for, if the kind treatment accorded me by the people I interviewed is normal. (They were chiefly people at the Greater London Council; at the Ministry of Transport; and at the London School of Economics; but elsewhere in London, too; and in Exeter—though that branch of my inquiries is not represented in the present book.) Nevertheless, in the end, I think that all of the several reconstructions that I offer of the debate over traffic congestion are governed by the documents I cite and are fitted to them in ways that would, I think, have occurred to other people with the same sort of ambitions of making sense of them, with or without the interviews, provided that they had selected the same data; and I suppose that in this case as in others to which the approach I illustrate in this book could be taken there might be principles and procedures of selection that would help as much as my interviews helped me. I hope it is clear that this methodological thesis does not in the least abate or qualify the thanks that I owe the people whom I interviewed; I myself—a philosopher grappling for once at first hand with the mixed pleasures of fact-finding—could hardly have dispensed with the interviews. I am grateful also for the comments that people who have seen or heard the results of my studies at various stages have made to me; and I must thank for financial support, besides the Canada Council, the Dalhousie University Committee on Research and Development in the Humanities and the Social Sciences, and, earlier, the John Simon Guggenheim Memorial Foundation.

D.B.

Halifax, Nova Scotia

1 Aims of the present study: chiefly, to illustrate the issue-machine approach

One way—not the only way, not the best way, not even by itself an adequate way—of looking upon a political system is to look upon it as a machine, or collection of machines, for processing issues. Suppose various policies *a*, *b*, *c*, *d*, etc. are proposed as alternatives to one another. Then they form an *issue*, *a* v *b* v *c* v *d* v etc., where 'v' stands for the non-exclusive sense of 'or' (since several proposals might be adopted simultaneously). Regarded as an issue-machine, the political system, or some part of it, will process the issue, by applying to each of the policies proposed various tests. For example, it will ask of *x*, any of the proposed policies, Tx?—does *x* have some property T (say the property of being inexpensive)? If the answer is 'Yes,' the policy in question may be advanced toward adoption, while if the answer is 'No,' the policy may be rejected then or there, or at least suffer a setback in its cumulating score. After all such tests have been applied at every station or location in the machine, there will either be a certain output of adopted policies; or all the proposed policies will have been rejected, in which case there will be a dead issue.

The test-questions Tx? Ux? etc., and the rules followed in disposing of the policies according to the results of each test, together with instructions for making sure that every policy has been put through every relevant test, form a *program*, of a sort that could be run on a computer. A computer working through such a program, if the program were one founded on evidence from real-world politics, would be *simulating* the workings of a political system (or of part of one). Hence the issue-machine approach has some affinities with systems analysis—with the application of cybernetic ideas to the description of politics in the manner of Easton or Deutsch.[1] My conception of the issue-machine approach, however, is much more directly akin to some of the work fostered by Simon and colleagues of Simon's on the simulation of decision-making routines in formal organizations.[2]

I by no means exclude larger questions about feedback, adaptation, and system-maintenance from the outer reaches of the issue-machine approach. With those large questions one might seek explanations of how issue-machine programs come to be established, acquire various features, persist or vanish; or one might inquire into the adaptiveness or maladaptiveness of using such programs for the issues assigned them. But the first things to be done on the issue-machine approach (I think) concern not such larger questions, but the smaller questions of identifying the programs that are in use and the networks of participating people and organizations that in one way or another institutionalize the programs.

These smaller questions bring to the center of the stage questions about the content of issues; the content, timing, and weight of reasons for or against various proposals; the recurrence or non-recurrence of certain sequences of reasons; the stability, or lack of stability, in the sequences of participation by various stations in the underlying networks; the biases of issue-determination resulting from all these factors. The smaller questions thrust to the side questions that have enjoyed a good deal more attention from political scientists: questions about personalities, interests, roles, offices, classes, competition, voting, power. Those questions are not going to fall out of fashion; the issue-machine approach thrusts them to the side without prejudice as to their interest and importance. They will continue to have their own interest and importance; moreover, together with the larger cybernetical questions, they will contribute to explaining the origin, operation, modification, and persistence of issue-machines. But first the issue-machines have to be identified and described.

Just how they are to be described, if they are to be described adequately for scientific purposes, depends on discovering which of their features have significant effects on their operation and output. The question just how cannot be settled in advance. Yet one needs something like a tentative answer to start work on the issue-machine approach. For how shall we identify any issue-machines if we do not have any notion of how they are to be described? Speculating about possible variations in issue-machines brings some features to light that could be used in describing and identifying issue-machines in actual political systems; but as I discovered when I tried it, purely *a priori* speculation on the subject is likely to get lost in a jungle of proliferating philosophical distinctions. A more promising way of going about the job of outlining a tentative answer as to how issue-machines are to be described is to take up some actual train of political events and consider certain variations in the issue-machine idea as so many possible ways of representing those events.

I adopt this way of doing things—subordinating speculation about possible descriptions of issue-machines to a series of attempts to describe an actual train of political events—in the present book. The actual train of events treated has to do with traffic congestion in the United Kingdom, and consists of pronouncements and actions on this subject occurring between the years 1963 and 1968. Policies affecting London happen to be centrally important to actions of the British national government on traffic: The problem of congestion is more salient in London than elsewhere, and the national government has tended not to act on this subject until it can act in accord with the government of Greater London. (Indeed, during the period in view in this study, it shared responsibility with the latter for traffic policy in the conurbation.) I shall be trying to take both governments into account, and as well a number of participants operating (sometimes or always) in positions outside the two governments: economists; town planners; motorists' and motor industry organizations.

The two governments are too loosely connected to be considered one formal organization; when the outside participants are taken into account as well, the notion of dealing with one organization must recede even further from mind. Yet possibly there is one issue-machine for traffic policy. I take it that besides being question-begging in this instance, making the presence of one issue-machine a necessary and sufficient condition for there being one formal organization runs counter to criteria for organizational identity such as source of funds, control over their expenditure, control over recruitment and promotion, ultimate accountability to a certain membership or public. Furthermore, association in one issue-machine for one subject of policy need not imply association on other subjects.

To be sure, the circumstances I have in view are less favorable for finding one issue-machine than the circumstances of dealing with the operations of one formal organization. But my choice of less favorable circumstances is deliberate. With the work foreshadowed and inspired by Simon (and by Simon and March) to follow, I would not expect to have much trouble in principle in finding an issue-machine (or machines) bounded by a formal organization that dealt continually with one or another field of issues. The most interesting question about the scope and future of the issue-machine idea is, Can it be applied where the participants are not all occupying assigned roles in one formal organization?

The chief aim of the present book, then, is to explore and illustrate possible versions of the issue-machine idea in the course of trying to apply that idea to the description of certain actual political events. This aim may be accomplished if none of the versions turns out to apply more than very tentatively: My main uses for the empirical data I have collected are in the way, first, of stimulus, and, second, of check, during the elaboration of a scheme of classification or description. In fact, I think, the versions that I shall consider all apply sufficiently well for each to be illuminating; and taken together, the weaknesses of one compensated for to a degree by the strengths of another, they accomplish a second purpose: In the course of indicating what case-histories would look like done on the issue-machine approach, I give a case-history of policy-formation on traffic congestion. Few subjects test the capacity of democratic government to protect civilized life more acutely; on few subjects can there be a more poignant gap between the broad concerns and subtle ideas of expert consultants and the conceptions and desires of the majority of voters. The majority of voters treasure the idea of themselves as car-owners—car-owners already or car-owners in prospect.

2 Changes in the context of traffic policy discussion, 1963–8

Before enumerating the variety of proposals bearing upon traffic congestion and beginning to discuss the issue-machine programs that may be supposed to have sorted them out during the years 1963–8, it will be helpful, I think, to give a brief sketch of the changing context of discussion in those years and incidentally justify taking those years as a period of study. It is a period marked at the beginning by a Ministry of Transport pamphlet, *Parking—The Next Stage*,[1] which reflects the established success of previous measures of parking control and looks forward to wider use of it, now consciously as an instrument for regulating the quantity of traffic coming into the central city rather than as a service to motorists; marked also, and more dramatically, by the appearance of the Buchanan Report, *Traffic in Towns*.[2] The period ends with the end in the Greater London Council of a unified bipartisan accord on traffic policy. What the end of this accord presaged as to future traffic policy I shall not inquire; I simply note that the change is remarkable enough to raise questions about the continuity of attitudes toward policy that did in fact prevail in the period selected.

In the local elections of April 1967, the Tories won control of the Greater London Council from Labour; but for a time—until late in 1968, in fact—the two parties remained in agreement on the chief points of policy respecting automobile traffic. The agreement was less stable on the Labour side; but Labour, like the Tories, were officially committed to heavy investment in road construction, in particular to the construction of the 'Motorway Box', a system of four ring roads successively farther from the center of London. After the GLC formally superseded its predecessors, the London County Council and the Middlesex County Council, in April 1965, the Labour majority on the GLC brought forward plans for the Motorway Box.[3] The Box and other roads were not expected to accommodate the whole of the tremendous increase in traffic to be inferred from projections of vehicle ownership by the Road Research Laboratory and by the London Traffic Survey.[4] But both parties, in 1967 as well as in 1965, took the position that congestion could be kept within tolerable limits by combining with road construction further measures of traffic management and extended control over parking.[5] In this belief they were strongly supported by the energetic staff of the GLC Highways and Transportation Department, the head of which had been inherited from the LCC, as had several members of Council active on traffic questions. The Labour party, while in opposition in Parliament, had striven to give the projected GLC more comprehensive powers (*vis-à-vis* both the Ministry of Transport and the borough councils).[6] The GLC, once inaugurated, strove to get them. The powers (e.g., to direct borough councils to set up and operate on-street parking schemes and to license the provision of publicly available off-street parking facilities publicly or privately owned) were finally obtained, as announced in a White Paper of 2 July 1968,[7] by a Tory Council from a Labour government. The same government had encouraged the Council to extend the area in which on-street parking was controlled to the full forty square miles of the Inner London Parking Area (instituted 1966), a measure directly responsive to the chief problem about growth in traffic congestion, which is the spread of congestion rather than increase in its intensity.

Under the Labour government, the GLC was also persuaded not merely to coordinate its policies for automobiles with policies for public transport but also to take responsibility for London Transport (in other words, of the major share, though not the whole, of the provisions for public transportation in the region).[8] With no sign of dissent from the Labour side of the Council, the GLC, illustrating another mode of extending or intensifying parking control, reversed in May 1968 the policy of requiring a generous minimum of parking accommodations in new office buildings;[9] and it mentioned the possibility of having to control existing accommodations even where these were not open to the general public. But in the fall of 1968, the Labour side of Council broke with the Tories on the Motorway Box; those Labour members who had long been inclined to stress housing more, relatively to roads, than their leadership on the Council, had found an argument carrying the whole side with them in the threat posed by the North and South Cross Routes of the Motorway Box to certain working-class neighborhoods.[10]

During this period, the Ministry of Transport exercised its

powers over London traffic in fair harmony with the GLC; there may have been gaps and omissions in planning, and some duplication of effort, but the Ministry on the whole supported the policies that the GLC favored. There was little or no visible conflict. (The visible difficulties about GLC powers had to do mainly with the boroughs and not so much even there with actual opposition as with procrastination.) This support was offered equally by a Tory government to a Labour Council and by a Labour government to a Tory Council, though a budget squeeze ruled out extra funds, e.g., for traffic wardens. The change in government may have made a marginal difference to the vigor with which the Ministry sponsored proposals going beyond the GLC program. Two major investigations of more radical policies were commissioned under the Tory government by an exceptionally active Minister (Ernest Marples). One of them was published while Marples was still Minister—the Buchanan report, already cited, *Traffic in Towns*, according to which unrestrained growth in vehicle ownership could be reconciled with the attainment of decent environmental standards only by massive reconstruction of the cities, late in 1963. *Cars for Cities*,[11] intended by Marples to complement Buchanan's inquiry into adapting cities to cars by inquiring how cars might be adapted to cities, appeared, without any show of enthusiasm on the part of the then Minister (Barbara Castle), in 1967, under the Labour government. The Labour Ministers of Transport (successively Fraser, Mrs Castle, Marsh) did not display much enthusiasm for following up the Buchanan report either; but a Tory government, too, even in financially less stringent times, would have boggled at the scale of expenditures that adapting cities called for; and there was strong resistance among Tories, too (on the GLC, for example)[12] to the sort of overhead road network that according to *Cars for Cities* would alone make the advantages of specially small 'city-cars' substantial.

The Labour government, though it did not so actively foster innovative thinking about traffic policy, did show somewhat more favor than the Tory government had toward full road-pricing, a proposal for attaining an economic optimum of traffic by keeping off the road drivers not willing to pay the full costs of being there (including the costs they impose, in congested conditions, on other drivers). This proposal, to which several economists had given voice individually in the years immediately preceding, was given full-dress ventilation in a report prepared and published under the Tory government—the Smeed Report, published in 1964.[13] The report, however, was inspired not by Marples, who gave it a very lukewarm reception,[14] but by Ministry of Transport staff, prodded rather strongly by outside advisers (drawn from the ranks of those same pioneering economists).

The road-pricing idea, given Marples' attitude, might have been neglected completely under a continuing Tory government except for some nursing by Ministry of Transport staff. Under the Labour government, the Ministers (especially Mrs Castle) joined the staff in fostering the idea, though the fostering was screened whenever it seemed advisable behind talk about technical difficulties still under investigation respecting instrumentation.

The Labour government went along with proposals for increased road-construction; indeed it spent a good deal more on road-construction than the Tories had, with annual expenditures on new construction and major improvements rising from £141·4 million in 1963 to £275·9 million in 1967.[15] Like the GLC, it put its reliance for the time being on traffic management and parking control as means of restraining traffic, so far as means of restraint were necessary; so much can be gathered from the review of proposals, *Better Use of Town Roads*, published in 1967.[16] But as that review also indicated, there were people at the Ministry who favored road-pricing as a more rational means; whereas the attitude of the GLC throughout the period was that road-pricing would be acceptable only if traffic management and parking control proved insufficient. The pressure groups representing motorists and the motor-car industry took an even stronger line, denouncing road-pricing as an intolerable extra 'tax' as soon as it was first proposed, though there were occasional indications that it might be made acceptable if other taxes on motorists were remitted and more of the money raised by taxes on motorists were put into road-construction.

3 The full list of proposals; and an issue-machine sketch of their fate

During the period 1963–8—more exactly, the period between the publication of the pamphlet *Parking—The Next Stage* by the Ministry of Transport in July 1963 at the beginning, and, at the end, of the publication in May 1968 of *A Parking Policy for London* by the Greater London Council, the following proposals were the chief ones considered in the United Kingdom as possible policies for dealing with traffic congestion (and the growth of traffic congestion), especially in central London:

P–a: Intensify parking controls.

P–b: Institute full road-pricing.

P–c: Adapt cities to heavy automobile traffic by extensive use of 'traffic architecture'.

P–d: Build new roads and road networks, in much greater amounts than already planned.

P–1: Let congestion take care of itself (treat it as a self-regulating phenomenon).

P–2: Charge for (a) special licences or (b) supplementary licences or (c) tolls or (d) daily admission tickets as condition of entry into congested areas.

P–3: Intensify traffic management measures other than parking controls.

P–4: Directly (e.g., by rationing) limit number of motor cars or growth in number (generally).

P–5: Directly limit number of motor cars owned in congested areas.

P–6: Find new means, build new systems of urban transportation.

P–7: Improve public transport and attract as passengers people who would otherwise use cars.

P–8: Multiply efforts to stagger working hours.

P–9: Intensify efforts to disperse offices and industries.

P–10: Shift goods traffic to other hours, routes, destinations.

P–11: Ban all motor traffic, or whole classes of traffic, from entering city centres (congested areas).

Regardless of their potential importance, not all of these proposals were considered at length. P–4 (direct limitation on number of cars owned) was not even (so far as I can see) seriously proposed: It was simply mentioned as an unthinkable suggestion in the Crowther committee's preface to the Buchanan Report; and immediately dismissed.[1] The Buchanan Report itself, moreover, was worked up and received on the assumption that not only would there not be any attempt to reduce the number of motor vehicles already present in the United Kingdom—that number (10·5 million in 1962, more than doubled since 1952,[2] without the doubling ever having been the intended object of any public policy) would simply be accepted; there would be no attempt, either, to check or even directly control the rate of growth in the number of motor vehicles. There could be no clearer illustration of the abdication by government from responsibilities for rational planning in the face of the impact of technological change. Yet the participants were by no means fully and constantly aware of the abdication. They tended in fact to speak as if the object of policy was to 'reduce traffic congestion' when realistically considered (in the face of expectations that the number of vehicles would rise to over forty million by 2010) the most that the government (or anybody else with an effective voice in making policy) contemplated doing was something that would moderate the growth of congestion. (The figure of over forty million represents a 'saturation point', but only in the sense that with that number of vehicles, every family in the country would have as many cars as it wanted, conformably to American standards; thereafter the number of vehicles would continue to increase simply as a function of increasing population.)[3]

The amount of attention received by other proposals in the list was in every case more substantial, but still very variable. P–2 (special licences, etc.) is given in a form that indicates how it was broken down for detailed examination; each of the particular proposals into which P–2 was thus broken down got attention comparable in amount to the attention received by several proposals that I have listed separately and done so because the principles which they involve seemed sufficiently distinctive—sometimes (as compared to P–8, for example, or P–9) more attention. P–a (intensifying parking controls) might have been broken down in a similar way, since a good deal of detailed attention was given each of several particular modes of intensification. I do not show the break-down because later it will be convenient to treat all these modes together as one package; but even then it will be important to bear in mind that one of the important modes of 'intensification', in spite of a degree of verbal incongruity, is *extension* in space (the same controls imposed over a wider area); and another mode, somewhat less important, is extension in time (the same controls, including time-limits and rate of charging at meters, kept in force for more hours of the day, or for more days of the week). Other modes of intensification that were examined at some length during the period under study included the control of parking space in private buildings; and the adjustment of time-limits and charges both for on- and off-street parking space to equate demand with supply.

The last-named proposal appears to come close to approximating P–b, the proposal of full road-pricing; and indeed one can easily imagine how full road-pricing could be brought in as a next stage beyond careful pricing adjustments of this kind. But full road-pricing (under which cars would pay for moving as well as for parking) might also be thought of as a next stage beyond one or another of the particular licensing proposals figuring in P–2—for those proposals, too, involve charging prices for driving in congested areas. What is crucial in determining affinity with full road-pricing is the intention with which these measures are carried out. Equating the demand for parking space with the supply is (unless supply is deliberately limited) compatible with being ready to accept any amount of traffic congestion. Only full road-pricing, of all the proposals in the list, comes with a definite criterion (debatable though it may be, since it takes no account of effects on the amenities of congested areas or on people in their capacity as residents or pedestrians) of optimum traffic. Other proposals might be required to link up with an intention of approximating to this optimum before their affinity is conceded.

It will soon appear that the full list of proposals is too long to work with for my purposes in the present book, especially since it is important to those purposes not merely to consider how proposals were sorted out in the period 1963–8, taking the period as a whole, but also to distinguish rounds of discussion on the basis of which recurrent features of issue-processing can be discerned. (Thus I shall have to find space in a sense to repeat information; I shall need to minimize the amount of information that has to be repeated from round to round.) I shall concentrate upon tracing the fate of the four proposals at the head of the list—the lettered proposals P–a, P–b, P–c, P–d. Yet it is natural to ask how their fate compared with the fate of the other proposals on the full list? What happened to the other proposals, and why?

Without much difficulty a plausible program can be laid out to represent the reasons effectively invoked for or against each of the proposals in the list. The outcome of the program would correspond to the real outcome of discussion in the period if the two-part classification 'Approved' or 'Rejected' were applied to both. I shall not try to describe such a program here; I shall instead move right on to describing very briefly a somewhat more sophisticated program in which both outcomes and the reasons that led to them are given weights of various values.

The point of giving weights to outcomes lies in the possibility of thereby indicating degrees of rejection (or perhaps less interestingly, of acceptance). Some policies—for example, P–4, direct limitation of automobile ownership—are rejected utterly, without the remotest real chance of being adopted in the foreseeable future. Others—significantly, P–b, road-pricing, is an example in the present case—are put aside and nursed (by the authorities; by people in a position to make policy later) until a more favorable moment arrives. The weights or scores assigned to different rejected proposals might vary up and down according to necessarily rough but none the less intelligible estimates of the chances that the proposals concerned will be adopted in the future—say, within a dozen years from the time of the present outcomes. The weights or scores assigned to different accepted proposals might vary with estimates of the amount of enthusiasm and commitment with which they are adopted, which can be looked upon as a measure of the fullness with which they will be carried out as stated. But not only could accepted proposals be scored on a somewhat different basis from rejected proposals; the question whether they should be scored at all can be settled separately.

A plausible way of scoring the full list of proposals so as to represent the outcomes for the whole period 1963–8, is as follows:

P–a	(Intensify Parking Controls)	Score 25
P–3	(Intensify Traffic Management)	5
P–10	(Shift Goods Traffic)	5
P–7	(Improve Public Transport)	4
P–8	(Stagger Working Hours)	1
P–9	(Dispersion)	1
P–b	(Road-Pricing)	0
P–6	(New Systems of Transportation)	0
P–2	(Special Licences etc.)	−1
P–d	(Massive New Road-building)	−3
P–5	(Limit Number of Cars Owned in Congested Areas)	−5
P–1	(Take Care of Itself)	−10
P–11	(Ban All Traffic, Certain Areas)	−12
P–c	(Traffic Architecture)	−15
P–4	(Limit Number of Cars or Growth in Number)	−25

(Adopted=1 or more; Rejected=0 or less)

The scores that appear in this representation can hardly be held to be uniquely indicated. Although the scores are not entirely arbitrary even on a cardinal interpretation—P–4 is not only farther away from being adopted than P–b, it is many times farther away than P–2—other cardinal numbers would answer my crude intuitions about distance as well as these; I could not say why P–4 should not be scored −49 or −164 rather than −25. Moreover, other people as familiar with the vicissitudes of discussion during 1963–8 as I, or more so, might disagree about the ordering of some proposals. I have myself no very firm idea about where P–7 should be put among the adopted proposals of lower rank, and I am open to persuasion about the relative ranking of P–1 and P–11 (for example).

Nevertheless, the representation is not only plausible, but (I hold) reasonably descriptive of the fate of the full list of proposals; and in any case it can serve both to illustrate representations of its kind and illustrate one of the chief constraints that can sensibly be imposed on a program for representing the previous course of discussion. Such a program may reasonably be asked to produce the outcomes represented. Hence the order of the questions that appear in the program and the weights given to the answers need to be selected with this aim in mind.

Beginning with a simpler program designed to arrive at outcomes classified without scoring as 'Approved' or 'Rejected' I have in fact assigned weights and then tinkered with the weights with the aim of producing the outcomes given above; and obtained considerable success in this simpleminded venture. The program is too long to set forth here; and not in itself very interesting, since it is merely a list of questions, one passing a proposal on to the next without any break or deviation. Though the questions have been grouped under several successive heads, the order of the groups and indeed the order of the questions is immaterial to the outcomes. The heads do no more than help to classify sorts of questions present both in the program and in the actual discussion: questions about Overriding Political Considerations (e.g., unprecedented costs or immediate vehement public opposition, score —15 in either case); about General Moral Considerations (e.g., undue hardship to some people, hurting poor rather than rich, engendering contempt for the law, weighted, perhaps significantly, —1 in each case); about Final Political and Parliamentary Considerations (e.g., radical departure from precedents accepted by the public, score —4). The largest group of questions comprises those dealing with Issue-Specific Reasons, with a range from promising actual reduction in congestion (from what it otherwise would be), score +1 if 'Yes', —15 if 'No', and requiring the use of technical devices not currently available, score —15, to achieving an economic optimum respecting road use, score +15, by way of a number of questions with weights of —1 for 'Yes' and +1 or 0 for 'No' (or vice versa), having to do, for example, with aesthetic considerations, with vexatious administrative features, or with affronts to motorists' feelings that they already pay more than enough for road services.

One might question the weights given individual questions, although there is some substantial justification for the whole system of weights in so far as it leads to the specified relative scores for the outcomes. (A smaller current of justification may run the other way: One may be prepared to make some adjustments in the scoring for certain proposals to accord with a system of weights that works well in reaching the specified outcomes for other proposals in the list.) Two of the moves that I had to make in tinkering to reach the right outcome for P–b, road-pricing, were to increase the negative weight for requiring a technical device not currently available to −15; and to change the answer in the case of road-pricing to the question about there being precedents accepted by the public from 'Yes' to 'No.' Both moves (especially the latter) may seem more than a little bare-faced. However, the first may be justified by pointing out that it is in fact a drastic disqualification to require a device not available; and that this was in fact the consideration cited most often and most prominently as telling against the road-pricing proposal. It is true that the citation of this consideration (always or almost always by the Ministry of Transport) was more by way of pretext than by way of actual technical difficulty; it was politically inexpedient, not technologically infeasible, to produce a device before the time for road-pricing became ripe. Taking this consideration along with the others voiced in the discussion and represented in the program at its face value, however, a score of −15 seems reasonable.

How can the second move, changing the answer about there being a departure from precedent from 'Yes' to 'No' be justified? The change amounts to reversing oneself from saying that road-pricing would not be a radical departure to saying that it would be. I suppose that if there is a justification, it is this: It was uncertain on a trial run of the weighted program how this consideration bore upon the road-pricing proposal, though perhaps it did not become urgently uncertain until I discovered that by reckoning the bearing as favorable I was contributing toward the untoward result of having the road-pricing proposal 'Adopted', high on the list. But is it unreasonable to make the move in question in reaction to this discovery? The result of the trial run was in error; I went back to discover just what contributed to the error and found that the bearing of one or another consideration may have been misjudged. There is in fact considerable evidence that road-pricing has been looked upon as a great departure from precedent; even though (as we have seen) both parking control and licensing could be treated as precedents. Careful management of parking control in successive stages of intensification might in fact prepare the way for road-pricing; but the precedent will not be created in the public mind until road-pricing sheds the (unjustified) reputation of being an abstruse and speculative academic solution, an intellectual quantum jump away from common sense proposals.

4 Recourse to a simplified approach

I shall not pursue further the question of formulating a program to deal with the full list of proposals, showing with more or less delicate accuracy how the proposals were actually dealt with in the United Kingdom in the years 1963–8. The amount of information that would have to be displayed and discussed is not unmanageable in itself; but it is a substantial enough body to deserve a sizeable book to itself, if real progress beyond the report that I have just given is to be achieved. I cannot deal with that much information here and still accomplish the chief purpose of the present book, which is to illustrate the issue-machine idea as a new approach to case-studies of policy-making. It is an approach, I think, that will lead to more exactly-formulated case-studies in which intuitive decisions about inclusion, interpretation and weighting are made visible; I think it is also an approach that will cast case-studies into a form from which relatively precise comparative data can be extracted—so that case-studies of policy-making will have a chance to adding up comparatively in ways that facilitate the construction of theories, something that even the best case-studies are woefully far from doing at present. The first sort of advantage (formulation) could in principle be illustrated by displaying a program dealing with the full list of proposals as they were in fact dealt with in 1963–8, were it not for limitations of space, though the length of the illustration would be a disadvantage even for illustrative purposes, since the massed details of the illustration would overshadow those purposes and the discussion of them. The second sort of advantage (comparison) could not be illustrated by writing out one program for the period of 1963–8. I must have at least two programs, and consecutive ones, to illustrate fully even elementary points of comparison, because these include points about the stability of issue-machines over time. I can produce two consecutive programs for illustrative purposes by limiting attention to four proposals (P–a, P–b, P–c, P–d) and dividing the discussion carried on in the period 1963–8 (beyond which my data do not go) into two rounds.

That is what I shall do, even though in doing it, I feel some apprehension that I am making such a drastic simplification that I may be jeopardizing the whole enterprise of illustrating the distinctive features of the issue-machine idea and thus conveying a reasonably full impression of the kinds of scientific advances that the idea may promise. Some of those advances may have to do with perfections of fine detail; so far as they do, little can be shown of them here. For my simplifications do not stop at leaving out of account all the proposals on the full list except four.

With them I leave out various parties to the discussion and lots of considerations, including considerations relating to the proposals I have chosen to treat. Given this limitation on the intake of data, it has been easy to effect another simplification, equally drastic but maybe even more misleading. The logical apparatus that I shall use is childishly simple: Almost surely it does not suffice to show in detail the ins and outs of a complex dispute like the one I treat; and in fact one thing to be especially hoped for from the issue-machine approach is not only that it would use more complex procedures from ordinary logic to give an exact representation of the complexities of real disputes; it would also draw on specialized logics like the logic of norms[1] (explicating the logical character of policies) and the logic of questions[2] (explicating the logical character of issues). As an aspect of profiting from the opportunities of formalization opened up by modern logic, the issue-machine approach should formalize *issues* as questions belonging to the logic of questions and the alternative proposals which constitute those issues as sentences in the logic of norms. One would then be in a position to ask, among novel and I expect useful questions, about the political effects of the logical differences between 'whether-questions' (e.g., 'Is parking to be controlled by price or is parking to be controlled by regulation?') and 'which-questions' (e.g., 'Which method of pricing parking will be the most efficient in reducing congestion?'). Which-questions are the appropriate vehicles for economic thinking and for incrementalist approaches to policies. On the other hand, they demand more complicated programs (suggesting that issues formulated as whether-questions may often in practice be dealt with more expeditiously). One of my present simplifications is to exclude which-questions entirely from figuring as such in the programs to be set forth. I shall give some attention to their presence off-stage, in the implied circumstances that shape the programs, and hence do something to illustrate the complex mutual relationships between them and whether-questions, a matter, I think, of great importance in determining both individual thinking and group decisions about policy-questions; but I shall not give these relationships the systematic treatment that they cry out for. To do so would take me too far away from the concrete case-study, which I am presenting for its own sake as well as for illustrative purposes.

There may be some defense for the simplifications, beyond the fact that they seem indispensable if my present purposes, illustrative and otherwise, are to be carried out in my present space. One thing that I wish to illustrate is the possibility of constructing a useful case-study of a more exactly formulated kind on the basis of very limited data—for the most part, data in the public domain; and at the level of detail at which I shall be working, I have come to feel that the logic of policy-making is surprisingly simple. It does not involve the complications of which-questions and hence is not on the face of it incrementalist, being peremptory in program rather than meliorative. Incrementalist thinking may none the less determine the spirit and shape of programs operating even at this level; I am inclined to think that it does, but its operation is less straightforward logically than I might have expected.

The simplifications, furthermore, should not prevent my discussion from illustrating or foreshadowing in at least a minimally effective way the most basic points about the issue-machine idea, considered, first, as a method of expressing case-studies of policy making more exactly; and hence, as a method of facilitating the comparison of case-studies, whether (a) to see whether essentially the same process is gone through in subsequent rounds of discussion within the same systems or (b) to detect variations in the processes at work on different issues, or in different political systems. On the basis of such comparisons, one may hope to see new and interesting theories formulated and tested—theories, for example, about the extent to which the persistence of various features of issue-machines depends on there being some approximation or other of a comprehensive formal organization; or theories about the origins and foundation of biases of various kinds, including bias against giving reasonable weight to long-run considerations.

5 Two themes of a simplified approach: S-stability versus P-stability

One basic version of the issue-machine is stable for sequence of stations (S-stability) as well as stable in effective program (P-stability).

Imagine the course of public discussion on a certain topic (e.g., traffic congestion) divided up into successive rounds. Each round would begin with the circumscription of the current issue regarding the topic; there would follow the introduction of one or more particular proposals that fall within the terms of circumscription; then a sequence of reactions to these proposals, followed by reactions to these reactions, and so forth, may be supposed to ensue. Each round would end with an authoritative decision on the issues (which might be a decision to let the issue drop and do nothing)—with an Act of Parliament, or, in London, an official commitment of the Greater London Council; or, short of such acts, since they are not always necessary for changes in policy and are in any case foreordained by party control of the legislature, by the publication of a White Paper or a committee report approved by the GLC.

The issue-machine (if there is one) at work upon the given topic is S-stable if the same stations—people holding certain recognized positions (as officials; experts; group leaders) or collections of such people, whether formally organized agencies or merely working alliances of interested people and groups—operate in the same sequence in each successive round. The issue-machine is P-stable if, regardless of which stations act in which sequence, in the end the same reasons count with the same weight for or against the proposals that happen to be introduced. S-stability does not entail P-stability, nor does P-stability entail S-stability. One might expect S-stability to provide an institutional basis for P-stability, however; and if P-stability exists without such a basis, it is more remarkable.

5.1. An S-stable machine

Making use of a simple symbolism, the basic features of which I have already introduced (at the very beginning of the book), I shall presently set forth a brief schematic representation of the discussion between 1963 and 1968 of four proposals regarding traffic policy. The representation will manifest S-stability; and, as it happens, P-stability, too. Before I give the schematic representation, I propose to give a prose account of the discussion—an account drastically abbreviated, like the representation to come, in respect to the selection of data, but amplified sufficiently to characterize matters which the schema will only indicate by symbols: namely, the identity of the stations, proposals, and reasons that figure in the discussion. (I shall also be introducing some further symbols and making points about the character of the symbolization.)

5.1.1. *First Round: History* The first round of discussion began, I hold, in July 1963 with the publication by the Ministry of Transport of the pamphlet, *Parking—The Next Stage*. But prior to or simultaneously with that event the current issue was circumscribed in such a way as to give at least a minimum of coherence to the ensuing discussion. Identifying such a measure of circumscription is not only helpful, perhaps indispensable, to arriving at a reasonably simple representation; in the present case, the circumscription can be recognized in explicit statements recurring throughout the discussion in both rounds. The circumscription might be represented as the result of a sequence of discussion, which might in real time have preceded the observed sequence. We need not, however, assume anything about the circumscription phase (Phase A) actually occurring; it suffices that during the discussion which does really occur all stations (all parties to the dispute) persist in viewing the issue as so circumscribed.

The way *issue-circumscription* operated in the present case may be described as follows: certain considerations P and Q lead the participants to hypothesize

$$(\exists x)\ (y)\ [(Fy \rightarrow y \neq x)\ \&\ Cx\ \&\ Nx],$$

i.e., that there is at least one policy not identical with any of the policies currently in force that (Cx) would entail some check to the growth of traffic congestion and that (Nx) would bring about net benefits not all of which can be expected from other policies in force or proposed. *P*, in the present case, was the belief that congestion is now and will continue to be intolerable for motorists and other road-users while planned road-construction remains unfinished; and *Q* was the belief that congestion is in fact likely to increase so as to outpace planned road-construction.

Then the issue-circumscribing question is the multiple-answer which-question,

$$? (\exists x) (Cx \ \& \ Nx) \ ?,$$

and given that every proposed policy is accepted as being Cx, the issue reduces to being circumscribed as some disjunction, modifiable without limit by addition or subtraction, of the form

$$Nx_1 \vee Nx_2 \vee Nx_3 \ldots . \vee Nx_n ,$$

which can be regarded as a multiple-answer whether-question. ('v'='or'.) Nx may be understood to imply needing to be adopted not just because of Cx (which is assumed for all alternatives) but because *x* satisfies whatever other conditions a participating station may wish to impose on accepting or rejecting a proposed policy. Some stations may have stringent specific conditions for concluding Nx; others may do no more than allude to P and Q, the issue-circumscribing reasons.

With the issue thus circumscribed, the actual events of the first round of discussion began, I wish to say, in July 1963 with the publication by the Ministry of Transport (one of the principal stations active in the discussion) of the pamphlet, *Parking—The Next Stage*. (I shall also count this event as the first in Phase B, the proposal-initiating phase.) The pamphlet reviewed experience (chiefly in London) with controls over parking, including the use of parking meters, and recommended a number of measures for making such controls more effective, chiefly on the ground, Sa, that the controls used hitherto had been successful by and large and accepted by the public. One distinctive feature of the proposed policy, *a*, of increasing parking controls, was that it called for a very large extension of the area in London in which parking spaces could be metered. The argument put forward by the Ministry of Transport could be represented as consisting of the premisses, Sa and Sa→Na, from which the conclusion was drawn, Na. (Simple arguments of exactly the same form occurred again and again through the discussion; I shall hereafter abbreviate them by giving only the shorter premiss and the conclusion, separated by three commas, thus: Sa , , , Na.)

The second event of Phase B of the first round was a speech given in Cambridge in August 1963 by Dr M. E. Beesley, then a research fellow in the economics of transportation at LSE.[1] Beesley was one of a number of economists who developed and pressed upon the Ministry of Transport a proposal for full road-pricing, *b*, according to which motorists would be asked to pay not only for their own costs but also for the costs (lost time, engine wear) they impose on other motorists in congested traffic. These costs vary with the amount of traffic; the road-pricing proposal accordingly envisaged adjusting the price charged motorists so as to achieve an economic optimum of road-use (more precisely, an optimum for motorists considered solely in that capacity). (The charges would be metered somehow while cars moved or parked in congested areas.) At any price higher than the optimum, so few motorists would use the roads that congestion costs would be lower than the price charged; at any price lower than the optimum, so many motorists would be attracted that congestion costs would rise above the price. At the optimum price, and only at the optimum price, every motorist willing to pay the congestion costs associated with the price, and no motorist unwilling to pay them, would be on the roads. Since there are congestion costs at present, and a zero-price associated with them, the introduction of a positive price would lead to fewer motorists using the roads than would otherwise.[2]

I shall treat Beesley and his fellow-economists as one station, in spite of their not being organized as a group, since they were throughout the period in close touch with one another, supporting each other's arguments and advocating (so far as proposal *b* went in the detail here considered) the same proposal. Several of them served in the Ministry of Transport or as consultants to committees appointed by the Ministry;[3] but their advocacy of *b* began and continued (among those at any given time outside the Ministry) without modification by these appointments. If we symbolize achieving an economic optimum among road-users as Ex, the argument of the Economists' Group may be given as Eb , , , Nb.

In November 1963, amid a spate of favorable comment from the press and various interested organizations, a comprehensive, elaborately prepared and lavishly produced report by the Buchanan Committee, on the future of traffic in towns[4] put forward views in which the approaches of civil engineers and city planners were combined. Although the report was sponsored by the Ministry of Transport, and was prepared while its chairman, Colin Buchanan, was still a civil servant,[5] Buchanan functioned throughout the whole period of discussion and beyond as an independent source of ideas; he was, moreover, by far the most frequent, articulate, and arresting spokesman for the ideas set forth in the report. I shall treat him as constituting a station all by himself. The message offered by station Buchanan, from the time of the report on, was that given the growth of traffic, the amenities of cities and towns could be safeguarded only by a policy, *c*, of creating by 'traffic architecture' a firm distinction between the primary road-network in each case and protected environmental areas; though the same object of safeguarding amenities, Ax, could be advanced by increasing parking controls, which would be necessary anyway. The report kept a hair's-breadth away from recommending either policy *c* or *a* in so many words: It confined itself, literally, to saying that *if* motor vehicles were to increase in the United Kingdom without any attempt to limit ownership and *if* it was desired both to afford accessibility and to safeguard the amenities of cities, then policy *c*, which in many cities would entail very large amounts of reconstruction, supplemented by *a*, would be needed. The recommendation of the report was thus hypothetical only; but its effect was categorical. Buchanan and his committee were taken as saying, Ac & Aa , , , Nc & Na; and for simplicity's sake I shall represent him as saying this, in the last action to be included in Phase B of the first round.

The most prominent new activity in Phase C—the phase during

which the several stations interacted in responses to the proposals raised during Phase B—consisted of interventions by the Motor Groups, under which heading I shall treat as combined in one station the Automobile Association, the Royal Automobile Club, the British Road Federation,[6] and other groups with various interlocking committees and joint support from the motor-car industry and from road contractors and the suppliers of road contractors. The first intervention of these organizations, I shall say, consolidating several actions, began in July 1963, with an adverse reaction to the proposal of intensifying parking controls, *a*,[7] continued in September with a vehement attack on the proposal of full road-pricing, *b*,[8] and concluded in November with an expression of support for Buchanan's proposal for redesigning city accommodations for traffic, *c*.[9] Thus, in various statements and speeches, the Motor Groups argued first (Ra) that increasing parking controls would involve an increase, intolerable to motorists, of vexations from regulations and (Ia) that the same policy would interfere excessively with the circulation of motor-vehicles and with access to the destinations of their users. Ra & Ia , , ,∼Na. Then the Motor Groups denounced the full road-pricing proposal, *b*, as (Bb) imposing an intolerable increase in the already excessive burden of taxation falling upon motor-vehicle owners and as (∼Wb) being unworkable, i.e., incapable of being carried out, even if it would check congestion were it to be carried out. Bb &∼Wb , , ,∼Nb. Without invoking any new reasons of their own or even (at this time) expressly agreeing with Buchanan's reasons (summed up by Ax), the Motor Groups affirmed Nc; they also kept up their perennial pressure (founded directly on P and Q, the issue-circumscribing reasons of Phase A) for *d*, a policy of building roads to an extent well beyond the road construction planned. Thus, Nc & Nd.

The Economists' Group made their strongest public bid for consideration in June 1964, with the publication of a report by a committee chaired by R. J. Smeed, which the Ministry of Transport had set up at the suggestion of members of the Group and which included some of its members. The report, *Road Pricing: The Economic and Technical Possibilities*, though far from receiving unqualified endorsement from the Ministry,[10] did give a thorough exposition of the theoretical argument for the proposal, calculated the benefits of applying the proposal to central London, and indicated, after reviewing various mechanical and electronic techniques for application, that the difficulties of these techniques were manageable. Eb , , , Nb.

The reaction of the Motor Groups to the Smeed Report was immediate and predictable, but concentrated this time on the financial burden argument, Bx. Bb , , ,∼Nb.[11] At about the same time (June and July 1964), the British Road Federation, a leading element in the Motor Groups, produced a pamphlet in which highlights from the Buchanan Report were combined with an urgent demand for substantial action on the lines of Buchanan's suggestions coupled again with the perennial Motor Groups demand for more road-building than planned.[12] This time, Buchanan's amenity arguments (Ax) were explicitly affirmed, with a stress on the need to separate vehicles from pedestrians. Ac , , , Nc; and Nd.

In April 1965, the Minister of Transport (then Fraser) crystallized a series of hints and hesitations which had begun under the previous government almost simultaneously with the publication of the Buchanan Report. The Minister said (Kc) that reconstruction of cities and towns as called for by those who demanded action on the scale of the problem set forth by the Report would require expenditures far beyond those that could be budgeted in the foreseeable future; and so (Kd) would meeting the demands of the Motor Groups for massive extra road-construction.[13] Kc & Kd , , ,∼Nc &∼Nd. In December 1965, the Minister of Transport (still Fraser) came out in favor of either increased parking controls or introducing road-pricing, without citing any new reasons (beyond the issue-circumscribing ones) for adopting them.[14] Na v Nb. There was an immediate reaction from the Motor Groups, which denounced the Minister's approach as 'negative' (specifically as failing to 'accept' motor-cars); leading spokesmen in the Conservative Party, and Grimond of the Liberal Party, joined in, even more vividly, but without adding any new grounds.[15]∼(Na v Nb) (which is logically equivalent to∼Na &∼Nb).

During the year 1966, the Greater London Council and the Ministry of Transport took, in the course of what I shall designate as Phase D, decisions which brought the first round to a close. In a pamphlet, *Parking Policy in Central London*, published in February 1966, the GLC announced the establishment of the Inner London Parking Area, extending the use of meters from eight square miles to forty; thus, it was adopting proposal *a*, and while the pamphlet did not specially stress the argument from success and public acceptance it says enough to justify imputing the argument to the GLC. Sa , , , Na. In June and July, one of the standing committees of the GLC expressed its opinion of *b*; road-pricing, the committee held, would (Ix) interfere excessively with circulation of motor-vehicles and access to the destinations of their users.[16] Ib , , ,∼Nb. Finally, in July 1966, the Ministry of Transport issued a White Paper, *Transport Policy*,[17] which endorsed *a*, without giving any specific reason; and rejected *b* for the time being, on the grounds that it was not yet technically feasible. Na; and∼Wb , , ,∼Nb.

5.1.2. *Second Round: History* Second rounds of discussion may begin with new actions; but they may also begin with the same actions with which the first rounds ended, and in such cases the rounds will be not only consecutive but overlapping. The difference is a difference in issue-machines; whatever importance it may have (possibly very little, though that cannot be settled *a priori*), it is a difference demanding notice in the present case; for the second round in the present case begins, after a presupposed Phase A circumscribing the issue in exactly the same form as before, with the same White Paper of July 1966 just cited as ending the first round. The White Paper looked both ways: retrospectively, it concurred with the adoption by the GLC of *a*, the policy of increasing parking controls with among other specific features the feature of extending the area of metered parking; prospectively, it recommended that *a′*, a policy of increasing parking controls yet further, be adopted. A distinctive feature of *a′* was the suggestion, paradoxical in view of previous attempts to give would-be parkers more chances to park, that parking accommodations in new central office-buildings be strictly limited to discourage office-workers from commuting in by car.

Thus the issue in the second round is in respect to circumscription exactly the issue in the first round, a fact in itself worth noticing, since it implies the issue in the first round was not in every sense settled: P & Q lead again to Nx_1 v Nx_2 v Nx_3 . . . v Nx_n? In view of this issue, the Ministry of Transport now advanced Na′.

The stations, proposals, and reasons that figure in the second round have now all been identified; so the sequence in which they occur can be described very briefly. In September 1966, Buchanan argued Ac & Ac′ , , , Nc & Na′ (several times over, in a speech at Dublin; in a commissioned article in *The Times*; in a speech to the International Road Federation).[18] The Economists' Group, in a book by D. J. Reynolds (immediately summarized in *The Times*),[19] came forward early in October 1966, to say reconstruction of cities and towns would cost too much, Kc , , ,∼Nc; but Eb , , , Nb. I assign one half (Eb , , , Nb) of this double event to the proposal-initiating phase; the other half (Kc , , ,∼Nc)—a response to Buchanan's proposals—to Phase C, the interacting phase. The rest of Phase C, in this round very brief, occurred later in October. First, on 16 October, Mrs Castle, the Minister of Transport, told a New York press conference that the Ministry was considering the introduction of road-pricing,[20] Nb; Ministry spokesmen hastened to say that *b* had not in fact been finally decided upon,[21] so the upshot of this intervention by the Ministry of Transport was, Nb or something else. Since the 'something else' can be reasonably identified, given the White Paper, with a′, the upshot may be rendered Nb v Na′. There was vigorous reaction from the Motor Groups—immediate comments on the press conference[22] were followed by a special meeting of the standing joint committee of the automobile clubs late in October[23] and a formal statement by the British Road Federation early in November.[24] They united in arguing Bb , , ,∼Nb.

Phase D, the phase of decision, began with a pamphlet, *Better Use of Town Roads*, published by the Ministry of Transport in July 1967 to review the discussion of traffic policy; this pamphlet acknowledged Eb but argued, at least for the time being, ∼Wb , , ,

~Nb; Na′. In effect, it recommended a′ residually, *faute de mieux*; if a positive reason (beyond the issue-circumscribing ones) were asked for, there is some basis for attributing Sa′ to the Ministry, partly on the basis of the pamphlet, but more as an inference from the political difficulties raised by *b* and other policies. But in fact the pamphlet stressed the novelties associated with a′, in particular the proposed restrictions on private parking accommodations which included the reversal in respect to provisions in new office buildings. In December 1967, the Ministry of Transport published another White Paper, *Public Transport and Traffic*,[25] in which Na′ was advanced directly upon the issue-circumscribing grounds P and Q and Sa′ is at best implicit. Sa′ became unmistakably explicit only with the GLC pamphlet of May 1968, *A Parking Policy for London*, which argued Sa′ , , , Na′. The round thus ended, as did the first round, with concurrence between the Ministry of Transport and GLC and adoption of a similar policy, eschewing road-pricing, and as well, reconstruction of cities and extra road-building, in favor of increased parking controls.

5.1.3. *S-stable Schema for the Two Rounds* An S-stable schema for the two rounds of discussion just described will be found laid out in symbolic form in Fold-out II which is at the end of the book. At this point, and during the discussion to follow, the reader will find it convenient to refer to the fold-outs continually.

5.1.4. *Some Virtues and Defects of the S-stable Representation* Anyone acquainted with the course of discussion on traffic congestion in the United Kingdom in recent years might well be inclined to say intuitively that the discussion had gone through a number of rounds and had taken much the same course in each round. The preceding schema, manifesting S-stability (and P-stability as well), makes this intuitive comment concrete and explicit (though no doubt it does so in only one way among a number possible); and it does show (selectively) just what each station characteristically contributed to the discussion and how these contributions impinged (or failed to impinge) on the fate of the four chief policies proposed.

It is a remarkable fact that one can go so far toward claiming both S-stability (for sequence of stations) and P-stability (in reasons and the weight given them) for the discussion of traffic congestion during this period. For during the two rounds considered, major changes occurred in the ultimate decision-taking authorities concerned with the issue. During the first round, a Labour Government succeeded the Conservatives at Westminster, in 1964; and the Greater London Council was instituted in place of both the London County Council and the Middlesex County Council, simultaneously with a major redivision and consolidation of the London (and Middlesex) boroughs (April 1965). During the second round, the Labour Party lost its initial majority on the Greater London Council (April 1967). Yet evidently the issue-machine for treating the subject of traffic congestion remained much the same, which supplies some grounds for skepticism about the importance in this connection of the changes in institutions and party control. Indeed, in general, S-stability and (even more) P-stability in the various issue-machines embraced by a political system suggest themselves as essential points to consider in reckoning how consequential even the most sweeping institutional changes may be.

In the schema, S-stability is already apparent as regards showing the Ministry of Transport, the Economists, and Buchanan acting in Phase B of both rounds; the Motor Groups and Ministry of Transport, in Phase C; the Ministry of Transport and the Greater London Council, in Phase D.

There are some variations in sequence in Phase B and Phase D between the two rounds that are easily eliminated by approaching the schema on a higher level of generality. The schema shows the Economists operating before Buchanan in Phase B of the first round and Buchanan before the Economists in Phase B of the second; we may, however, find stability in the fact that *either* the Economists *or* Buchanan operated after Phase B was begun by the Ministry of Transport (and then whichever had not operated operated in turn). Similarly, in respect to Phase D the claim for stability must be rendered, *either* the Ministry of Transport *or* the GLC operated, once or twice; and then the other station, once or twice. But this simple-minded artifice for Phase D can be backed by a significant observation: rounds of discussion on traffic congestion in cities close (one might even hypothesize, close for the whole of the United Kingdom) when the GLC, which has the most salient congestion troubles to deal with, adopts a policy with which the Ministry of Transport is in public accord.

Phase C requires somewhat more elaborate treatment if the claim of S-stability is to be carried through on the basis of the schema. Operation (5) in the second round, by the Ministry of Transport, can be looked upon as paralleling Operation (8) by the same station in the first round; then Operation (6) by the Motor Groups in the second round matches Operation (9) by the same station in the first. But we have four operations left over, which occur in Phase C of the first round but which are not matched by anything visible in the schema in Phase C of the second round: Two of these operations are by the Motor Groups; one by the Ministry of Transport; and one by a station—the Economists—that appears to operate in Phase C of the second round only by dividing up the action also represented as Operation (3) of Phase B.

Given the schema, there are at least three possible ways of saving the claim of S-stability in the face of this discrepancy. One might find further operations to fill the gaps in Phase C of the second round. Or one might treat the second round, which does after all run off in a shorter time as an abbreviation of the first—a shorter version, which might be supposed likely to occur every now and then, perhaps at regular intervals, during the succession of the rounds. Or one might treat the second round, especially in respect to Phase C, as a projection or condensation of the first, in which the actions of the first round reverberate even if they are not explicitly repeated. The Ministry of Transport does not need to repeat Kc , , , ~Nc; other participants will remember this action from the first round; in fact the persistent influence of Kc is manifested by the repetition of the reason in the second round by the Economists' Group, in Phase B. But one might also impute persistent influence to Kd, invoked by the Ministry of Transport in the first round; and to the complex of reasons advanced by the Motor Groups against *b*, road-pricing, in the first round, including ~Wb, its supposed unworkability, which becomes explicit in Phase D of the second round, just as it was in Phase D of the first.

Clearly there are some dangers in pressing the notion of projection very far. Instead of imputing Rx & Ix to the Motor Groups as reasons opposing *a′*, the new version of increased parking controls, one might wonder whether the absence of Ra′ & Ia′ , , , Na′ from the schema did not signify an inclination on the part of the Motor Groups to abandon the fight against parking controls in order to concentrate their attack upon road-pricing. At the moment, I am not concerned with inquiring into this possibility, but simply with making the opposite point that the discrepancy at issue may be no more than an adventitious and insignificant qualification to a claim of S-stability based on the schema.

There are other weaknesses in the schema that may run deeper, since they involve the very method of constructing it. The identities between reasons, actions, and indeed between proposals appearing at different places in the schema are identities resting upon judgments by the author of the schema that reasons, actions, and proposals expressed in different ways are substantially the same things. But this sort of simplification is indispensable whether or not its particulars are defensible in the present instance; without it we would have little or no use for general concepts of any kind, certainly in a first report; though in principle the report should of course be replicable. More questionable, perhaps, is the simplification achieved by consolidating several actions or operations at different times under one head: e.g., a number of actions, occurring over several months, by the Motor Groups under Operation (4) in the first round; three actions by Buchanan under Operation (2) in the second round. This simplification is justifiable (if at all) only on the empirical ground that the actions brought under the consolidated heads would in fact have been backed by the stations concerned simultaneously at any time during the period from the earliest action to the latest. This justification could be undermined by evidence that later actions in either of the consolidated series were influenced by operations in-between other stations; and in other ways.

The schema given is highly simplified in yet another respect. All sorts of intimately relevant matters have been left out of account. The schema does not mention all of the policies proposed in the United Kingdom during the period 1963–8 for dealing with traffic congestion; nor does it mention all of the reasons advanced for or against particular policies. For example, it does not give any space to proposals (to be found on the full list given earlier) for monorails or for overhead road-networks to accommodate tiny 'city-cars'; it does not include the objection to road-pricing that it would jeopardize privacy (because enforcement might require keeping track of people's movements) or the objection that the policy would apply in places where it was not needed, if it was applied all over the country, and single out London for invidious special treatment, if it was not. During the period covered by the schema, the GLC put in a lot of time and energy struggling to acquire from the Ministry of Transport and the London boroughs greater authority over measures to deal with traffic congestion in London. There is no mention in the schema of this struggle, though it got perhaps as much political attention during the period as any of the measures specifically proposed and the efficacy of any measure adopted by the GLC may have depended upon its outcome.

These omissions, too, are to be justified (if at all) partly on grounds of expository necessity, which apply to every account whatever of human affairs. The present method simply makes more visible and hence more poignant the uncertainties of selection that are practised in every history and case-history. In part the omissions can be justified on the empirical ground that taking notice of them would not compel any revision in the entries already included in the schema. In fact, the schema as it stands already allows for some of these other matters. The case presented by the GLC for greater authority over traffic policy was based on the projections of congestion turned up by the London Traffic Survey; but the effect of those projections is allowed for in Phase A, during the circumscription of the issue. Agreement on the implications of these projections and of similar projections from other sources remained sufficiently constant through the period to maintain the issue in the form circumscribed. Questions were raised about exaggerations in the projections, for example, in Reynolds's book (*cf.* Operation (3), second round); but these questions did not lead to widespread doubts until after the second round closed. The doubts then contributed to the defection of the Labour side of the GLC from the road-plan for London on which both sides were agreed during the period of the schema. The event of defection, and the contemporaneous success of the GLC in extracting a larger grant of traffic authority at Westminster, do not challenge the implications of the schema. They raise questions instead about whether the S-stability of the schema continued for a third round, questions outside the scope of my present inquiry.

5.1.5. *Constructing a Program from the Schema* The schema manifests both an issue-processing network and, assigned to the stations operating in that network, a sequence of actions involving reasons. The sequence is not itself a program, but a program that would produce the items in the sequence, in the order in which they appear in the sequence, can easily be constructed from the sequence. It would be tedious, and enormously space-consuming, to write out such a program in full detail; but I shall give a sketch that will give a reasonably determinate idea of what its content might be.

Let us assume a computer in which a number of registers have been designated 'question locations' for the Ministry of Transport, the Economists, Buchanan, the Motor Groups, the Greater London Council respectively; others, designated 'public endorsement locations' for these participating stations; still others, designated 'public denunciation locations.' The program begins with Phase B and proposals *a*, *b*, *c*, and *d* as inputs and specific loadings in the question locations; it turns to the Ministry of Transport question location and asks the first question found there, 'Which if any of the input proposals is Sx ?', applying to each in turn a subroutine for determining Sx. (The subroutine would call up successful policies of traffic control past and present and compare features of these policies with a current proposal; if the current proposal had according to explicit criteria a sufficient number of sufficiently important features it would be held to be Sx.) The program instructs the computer to register any proposal that is Sx as Nx in the public endorsement location for the Ministry of Transport. Then, consecutively, it turns to the Economists' question location and the question location for Buchanan and registers any proposals that in the one case turn out to be Ex and in the other case Ax, in the public endorsement locations for the Economists and for Buchanan respectively.

The program opens Phase C by applying questions to be found in the Motor Groups' question location to any proposals now present as Nx in the three public endorsement locations so far used. The questions are, first, 'Is any of these proposals Rx or Ix?', with the accompanying instruction that if Rx and Ix, then ~Nx is to be registered in the Motor Groups' public denunciation location; second, 'Is any of these proposals Bx or ~Wx?', with the accompanying instruction that if Bx and ~Wx, then again ~Nx is to be registered in the Motor Groups' public denunciation location. (In step (6), Bx alone will turn out to suffice to have ~Nx registered there; so ~Wx may be regarded as redundant. But it need not be assumed that the program is ideally economical from a logical point of view; and ~Wx in step (4) recurs later in the sequence of events, with at least a hint of reverberation.) The questions from the Motor Groups' question location continue with the program asking whether any of the three proposals designated as Nx in public endorsement locations used in Phase B is Ax, prescribing that any such proposal is to be registered as Nx in the Motor Groups' public endorsement location. The appearance of Nd in that location may be accounted for by ascribing to the Motor Groups' question location a fourth question, 'Which if any of the original input proposals is Fx, i.e., conforms to past demands, not yet satisfied and not yet obsolete, of the Motor Groups?' with the appropriate accompanying instruction about registering Nx.

Now (as an effect of receptivity at the Ministry of Transport to the idea that the proposal should be fully investigated) the program gives the Economists a second chance to affirm *b* (road-pricing) as Eb. The program might be considered to run this way at this point: 'Clear the Economists' public endorsement location; then consider, "Which if any of the original output proposals is Ex?" Register any such proposal as Nx in the Economists' public endorsement location; and if there is such a proposal add to the list of questions at the Ministry of Transport question location the question, "Is any surviving proposal Ex?" and the instruction, "If Ex, then (Y v Nx) is to be registered at the Ministry of Transport public endorsement location"' (where 'Y' is a place-holder to be replaced by any formulas Nx already registered at that location). This second chance to affirm Eb may be supposed, besides having this effect on the Ministry of Transport's question location, to be distinctive in employing a more thorough sub-routine for determining Ex than was employed in Phase B.

Suppose the program alerted the Motor Groups' question location whenever during Phase C the public endorsement locations of any of the other participating stations manifested some activity. Thus when the Economists' public endorsement location was cleared at the beginning of step (5), the program prescribed that the Motor Groups' question location be visited in step (6). Once there, the program clears the Motor Groups' public endorsement and denunciation locations, then asks, 'Is any of the proposals in the public endorsement locations active in the last step Rx or Ix?' and gives the accompanying instruction to register ∼Nx in the Motor Groups' public denunciation location; then the program would ask, 'Is any of these proposals Bx?' with the accompanying instruction to register ∼Nx; and so on. In other words, the questions applied from the Motor Groups' question location in step (4) would be applied in order, with this difference, that if any determination such as Bx alone sufficed to imply ∼Nx (or Nx), the program would immediately register ∼Nx (or Nx) and move on; when the proposals in the public endorsement locations active in the step before had all been considered, the program would recall from storage any proposals that had been in the Motor Groups' public endorsement location before clearing at the beginning of the step and register them again; hence Nc and Nd reappear there.

At this point, the program brings in a question from the Ministry of Transport that has a decisive effect on the fate during this round at least of certain proposals: 'Is any proposal registered as Nx in the public endorsement location of any other station Kx (too costly)?', with the accompanying instruction, 'Register as ~Nx in the Ministry's public denunciation location and send any such proposal to the final output register as "Rejected".' Such proposals, in this case *c* and *d*, then drop out of the program so far as further consideration is concerned. In step (8), the Ministry of Transport question location is again visited, this time to call into play the question and instruction added as a result of the Economists' action in step (5). 'Is there any surviving proposal (i.e., not "Rejected" in a previous step) such that Ex?' with the accompanying instruction that has the effect of adding disjunctively any such proposal to any proposal already registered in the Ministry of Transport public endorsement location as Nx. Hence 'Na v Nb' now appears in that location instead of just 'Na' as heretofore.

The Motor Groups' question location having been alerted (as it was preceding step (6)) by the activity in one of the other stations' public endorsement locations, in step (9) the program runs through the same routine as in step (6), except that (as a result of the action in step (7)) *c* and *d* are dropped once they are recalled from storage, because they are seen to have been determined as 'Rejected.' The Motor Groups' public denunciation location registers finally only '~Na & ~Nb;' their public endorsement location is finally empty.

The overall aim of the program in Phase D, one may suggest, is to bring about concurrence between the Ministry of Transport and the Greater London Council. Either the GLC or the Ministry of Transport may initiate the phase—the program might fix upon which does so by resort to a chance device if it has no information on which to base a more specific criterion (I do not). If the GLC acts first, as it does in the first round, it asks of any proposals surviving on the public endorsement locations of any other participating stations, first, whether any of them are Sx, in which case the program goes on to have Nx registered in the public endorsement location for the GLC; it asks, as the second question (the final one, at least in this connection at this stage) produced from its question location, whether among those proposals any is Ix, in which case it is to be registered as ~Nx in the public denunciation location for the GLC. (Should the program rule out the possibility of one and the same proposal's being both Sx and Ix? But we need not suppose that the program is logically perfect, i.e., among other things, secure against falling into contradiction in any circumstances.) The program turns finally from the GLC question location to the question location for the Ministry of Transport (or vice versa, depending on the order followed in the given case). From this location it takes first the question, 'Is any of the proposals now registered in the public endorsement location of any participating station ~Wx?', with the accompanying instruction not only to register such a proposal as ~Nx in the public denunciation location for the Ministry of Transport but also to send it to the final output register as 'Rejected'. (We might also include in the program at this point a provision barring the adoption of any proposal registered in the GLC public denunciation location as ~Nx. The endeavor toward concurrence would thus have a more explicit representation.) The second question is, 'Is there any proposal that is registered both in the GLC public endorsement location and in the public endorsement location for the Ministry of Transport?' with the accompanying instruction to send any proposal to the final output register as 'Adopted'. With this question and instruction the program comes to an end.

Reconciling the sequence of actions shown in the schema for the second round with the operation of the program just constructed for the first round requires modifications in the program. It is only the program so modified that could plausibly be claimed to be P-stable; and as it will turn out, even so the claim may need to be qualified by ascribing to the program a capacity for self-modification. However, if that is the sort of program at work in the system, we would hardly wish to overlook its presence! Again, *ad hoc* tinkering brings into view a distinction perhaps of substantial importance.

In the second round, evidently, the inputs in the way of proposals consist of *a′* (*a*, renewed and extended), *b*, and *c* only; *d* does not appear. Except for a minor variation in the order of their operations, the same stations are visited to the same purpose in Phase B of the second round as were visited in Phase B of the first. In Phase C, however, the variations are more than minor: nothing at all appears in Phase C of the second round that corresponds to the action of the Motor Groups in step (4) of the first round or to the action of the Economists in step (5) of the first round or to the action again of the Motor Groups in step (6) of the first round. How is the absence of anything corresponding to these actions to be accounted for? Moreover, how is the fact that in the second round it is the Economists who affirm Kc (*d* not being in the running) and infer ∼Nc, not the Ministry of Transport, as in the first round?

Suppose that the result of the operation of the program in the first round was not only to adopt *a*, but to strike *a* or any similar policy of increasing parking control from the list of practical targets in view at one station or another. In effect, at least for the time being, the Motor Groups, for example, might be supposed to have abandoned any thought of attacking proposals for increased parking control in favor of more vulnerable targets. Accordingly, instructions might be ascribed to the program all along that would lead to such an outcome. Thus nothing like step (4) of the first round appears in the second round. (If the Motor Groups in fact had not abandoned the attack on *a* or *a′* or the like, the present device would not be a suitable feature of the program, even though nothing in the selected evidence to be reconciled with the program precludes its being a feature; but I continue with the device, as a simple illustration.)

A step corresponding to step (6) of the first round drops out of the second without a further modification of the program because no change occurs in the public endorsement location of any other station during Phase C until step (5), which does alert the Motor Groups station and leads according to the routine already sketched for its question location (together with the device ruling out *a′* as a practical profitable target) to step (6) of Round Two.

The absence of an action by the Economists to endorse (again) *b* in Phase C of the second round and the presence of an action by them denouncing *c* because it is found to be Kc, in lieu of this being done by the Ministry of Transport (as it was in the first round), presents more of an embarrassment. (It is an embarrassment, to be sure, that in part is only an effect of dividing up one and the same action of October 1966 to get both step (3) and step (4); and we might not scruple to enjoy simultaneously the advantages of taking this as one action, by repeating Eb , , , Nb in step (4), as well as the advantages of dividing the action so that we obtain step (3).)

The presence of Kc , , , Nc in step (4), rather than in a step taken by the Ministry of Transport, would still have to be explained, however; and there are illustrative benefits to be gained from dealing with the embarrassment in its full dimensions. The way to deal with it, inevitably, is to complicate the program. Given just these actions, and the program as sketched to date, one might, for example, suppose that the question location for the Economists listed a question Kx? after the question Ex? and the question location for the Ministry of Transport contained an instruction to skip Kx? if its previous answer (in the first round) remained unchallenged. The program might also contain a provision (one of several, perhaps, that had the effect of shortening second rounds) that Ex? need not be repeated at the Economists' question location in Phase C if it had been asked at that location in the round just preceding and mentioned again in Phase B of the present round.

The difficulty with such provisions is that it must be classed with the device eliminating attacks on *a′* in the second round as a self-modifying feature of the program, adapting the content of the program in one round to actions that occurred in the round previous. If it is not so strongly self-modifying as the other device, since it does not reflect the outcome of a previous round, it has the drawback of persistently embarrassing company. For why should the Economists ask Kx?, and the Ministry of Transport abstain from asking it, especially since the determination ∼Nx because Kx leads to 'Rejection' (in the second round as well as in the first), and for 'Rejection' one might demand the authority of the Ministry of Transport (or of the Ministry of Transport and the Greater London Council, acting concurrently)? I shall not try to paper over this crack, except to suggest that maybe one could take the presence of Kc , , , ~Nc in the sequence and the subsequent disappearance of *c* from among the proposals considered as evidence that Kx? and if Kx, then ~Nx had operated at the Ministry of Transport—echoing their earlier operation there, or this present just preceding action at the Economists' question location—though tacitly. (But that 'tacitly' is of course a bigger jump from the facts actually observed than anything I have yet tried.)

Phase D of the second round runs, with a minor variation in the order in which the stations are called upon that could easily be allowed for in the program, along lines exactly parallel to Phase D of the first, and with an equivalent outcome.

The program, with the anomalies removed by the devices I have suggested, has a drawback, *vis-à-vis* the schema from which the program has been constructed, of exaggerating the continuity of the discussion and the extent to which one station takes into account the actions and reasons of other stations. The schema makes the awkward possibility plain that for the most part the reasons given by one station are not heeded or repudiated at other stations—they are (in content) just ignored. I expect this phenomenon is frequently found in political discussions. It may significantly be contrasted with an ideal of logically full debate, in which every reason is confronted and criticized if not adopted by every station, with the criticisms in their turn being heeded or rejected with stated counterarguments. But the issue-machine idea should not be abused to suggest full debate when full debate has not occurred; it should be used, in this connection, to indicate how far the debate fell short of being full debate, and in exactly what respects.

5.2. Transition to (merely) P-stable representation

How important is the sequence of reasons after all, if at best other stations merely respond to them as signals for asserting or re-asserting their own unmodified views? What matters, it might be said, is not the sequence, but the contribution of the sequence to giving various reasons cumulative weights that in the end produce the observed output in adopted policies. One might well think that perhaps it would be simpler just to write out a program *ex post facto*, abstracting entirely from the temporal sequence of operations, and including just the questions that proved decisive.

Such an approach is not only feasible; it is simpler in the present case; and the evidence, considered soberly and cautiously, may be thought to support it somewhat better than attempts at S-stable representation. For the information that would be lost by shifting to such a program, manifesting P-stability at most—information about stability for the sequence of stations between the first round and the second—has, it must now be confessed, a somewhat shaky footing in the evidence.

The operations represented did occur in the order given; and most of the operations were important enough so that including them was not arbitrary. One could hardly be expected to ignore the Ministry of Transport or GLC pamphlets on parking; the White Papers; the Buchanan Report; the Smeed Report; or *Better Use of Town Roads*, a conscious effort to consolidate the discussion, even though it provoked little reaction. But other operations—e.g., Beesley's speech or Reynolds's book; even perhaps Mrs Castle's New York press conference, in spite of the especially vigorous reaction it evoked from the Motor Groups—are no more important than some operations left out.[26] If all operations with as strong a title to being included as one or another of these have were put into the schema, the present picture of S-stability might be obliterated.

In particular, it is important to realize that the GLC (or its predecessors, especially the LCC) was active throughout the period, at several levels: staff, committees, and members speaking at question-time made various pronouncements regarding traffic congestion. Buchanan was continually active during the first round, several times under the sponsorship of the Motor Groups, though Buchanan was too important a figure (as well as too self-sufficient) to become even for a moment merely a spokesman for the Motor Groups. There was recurrent advocacy of the road-pricing proposal by one or more of the people (or people and agencies, if we include the Institute of Economic Affairs)[27] belonging to the Economists' Group.

People who participated in the discussion had the impression that all the stations were continually operating on traffic questions and that every station was continually aware of the stream of operations issuing from every other (whether or not they chose to respond to those operations overtly). At least at the level of generality on which the schema is situated, the picture of sequence within the network of stations might be replaced with a picture of something like resonance (though I do not know what logical form such a picture would have).

It is true, the choice of a resonance picture is not wholly inevitable. Because the S-stable schema contains such a high proportion of indisputably important operations, its claim to accuracy is far from being empty; perhaps even its selection of less important operations can be defended as representative in a way that makes the schema genuinely illustrative of the course of discussion. Moreover, S-stability, lost with one wave of enrichment, might reappear in a more complex form if the schema included yet more operations—say, all of those with as strong a title as the weakest title of those now included.

So at worst giving up the claim of S-stability for the two rounds is giving it up without prejudice; and a more modest claim of stability may be pressed in its stead, namely a claim of stability in effective program only, P-stability alone. In this version of the issue-machine idea, a program for processing issues of a certain kind in form and content is ascribed to a political system. Behind the program, of course, there are men and institutions; it will remain to explain just how they are motivated and co-ordinated in such a way as to give effect to the program. Without S-stability, the explanation will be more urgently required; for it will now be more remarkable to have P-stability. Perhaps constancy in the membership of the set of participating stations suffices; but one would think that constant membership plus S-stability gave stronger grounds for expecting P-stability.

5.2.1. *A Simple Representation for P-stability Only* Abandoning any attempt to represent the actual temporal sequence, the program of reasons synopsized a moment ago can be rewritten to include only reasons that fall into a minimum set sufficient to bring about the observed output. There may be a number of such sets; one that is intuitively illuminating in respect to the reasons it includes and also illuminating in the way it repays discussion gives the following simple program: Assuming the issue circumscribed as in the A Phases of the schema, the program asks of every policy proposed,

Is the policy S (one that follows a successful and accepted precedent)?

Is the policy K (one that would require expenditures far beyond amounts that can be budgeted)?

Is the policy W (one that is workable immediately)?

then applies the rule,

If Kx or ∼Wx, then reject the policy, i.e., (finally) ∼Nx;

and if ∼Kx and Wx and Sx, accept it, i.e., (finally) Nx.

The results, corresponding to the observed output, are

Sa & ∼Ka & Wa , , , Na;

∼Sb & ∼Kb & ∼Wb , , , ∼Nb;

∼Sc & Kc & Wc , , , ∼Nc;

∼Sd & Kd & Wd , , , ∼Nd.

(See also Fold-Out III.)

Only *a* survives and only *a* becomes adopted policy. The program could be simplified further by omitting to mention Sx, and inferring finally Nx from (and only from) ∼Kx & Wx.

A program as simple as this one would still be worth noticing. It is an empirical fact that it fits either or both of the rounds of discussion observed, a fact that contrasts sharply with the possibility that the evidence might have required a much more complicated form. Even with the same number of reasons (here three) the form would necessarily be more complicated at the same level of abstraction if (i) the reasons were meliorative ones, each calling *prima facie* for the adoption of that policy which, compared with the alternatives, was best on some point of comparison (ii) provision had to be made for balancing a gain on one such point against a gain or loss on other points. Here by contrast Kx and

∼Wx function as peremptory reasons, which rule out a policy or favor its adoption on the basis of some property that can be ascribed without comparing it with alternatives; and Sx—the impact of which is unclear—counts simply in favor if it obtains and perhaps neither one way nor the other if it does not. It was very likely not a necessary condition of a policy's being adopted regarding traffic congestion.

Meliorative reasoning, it should be said, had an important impact on the discussion at the outset; for it was by comparing the burden of congestion with alternative difficulties that premiss P in the circumscribing phase was arrived at. Unchecked congestion would not have been considered intolerable if it had been felt that other things (housing, perhaps; perhaps a reduction in taxation) were so urgent as to preclude any serious attention to traffic problems. Again, meliorative reasoning may be supposed to operate after the discussion finished, to determine exactly how much effort—financial and otherwise—is going to be put into the policy adopted. Moreover, Kx, though it functions as a peremptory reason within the program, does so only because it has been assigned more or less firmly a cut-off point beyond which it rejects expenditures as beyond budgetary possibility; and this cut-off point reflects a meliorative comparison with other subjects calling for budgetary provision.[28]

5.2.2. *Revision of Representation Claiming P-stability Only* The simple program just given was, I would claim, stable through the first and second rounds. In the second round, it picked *a*′, on the same basis as it picked *a* in the first round. Simple as the program is, it is worth noticing; and its stability through two rounds makes it doubly so. But it is not, in fact, as illuminating as a slightly more elaborate program, which can be arrived at by reconsidering the effect and significance of ∼Wx. Was ∼Wx, invoked in Phase D by the Ministry of Transport, really the same reason as ∼Wx, invoked earlier by the Motor Groups? The Motor Groups, casting about for any convenient stick to beat a proposal that they disliked mainly for its prospective burden of charges (Bx), utter a vague charge without giving any detailed argument in support.

The Ministry of Transport, *au courant* both with the theoretical economic argument for road-pricing and with current experimentation under its own sponsorship with metering systems, particularized ~Wb as resting on the problem of finding a fully satisfactory metering system. Moreover, clearly the Ministry of Transport regarded Ex (attaining an economic optimum) as a good reason for adopting *b*; yet in the end the Ministry allowed ~Wb so much force as to overbalance this attraction.

If we take the apparent decisiveness of ~Wb at face value, yet allow for the attraction of Eb, the following program emerges, after Phase A:

Is the policy S or E?
Is the policy K?
Is the policy W?

with the rule,

If Kx or ~Wx, reject the policy, i.e. (finally) ~Nx;
and if ~Kx and Wx and (Sx or Ex), accept it, i.e. (finally) Nx.

(See also Fold-Out III.) So, we could infer, *b* would have been adopted, in spite of being ~S, if it had got over the ~Wx hurdle.

But was ~Wx a genuine hurdle? I believe (and not by any means I alone) that it was a mere pretext. The technological problems, if any remain, could be cleared up almost immediately the Ministry decided to commit itself to full road-pricing, though no doubt enough disadvantages could be found in any one metering system to give color to the description, 'not fully satisfactory.' (The first principle of political rhetoric: Some disadvantages can be found, given average ingenuity on the part of opponents, in any practical policy on any subject.)

~Wb, invoked by the Ministry of Transport, did not signify adoption by the Ministry of the Motor Groups' view of road-pricing. The Ministry continued its experiments; and it continued, from time to time, asserting Eb and describing *b* as the 'ideal' or 'most rational' solution. Nor should we suppose that the Ministry meant to pretend to a meeting of minds with the Motor Groups; the way it continued to nurse the road-pricing proposal publicly stands against this supposition, too, as does the tradition of British public administration, which is not one that lightly abandons its own public positions in favor of a pressure group's.

Yet ~Wb, invoked by the Ministry of Transport, does answer in a way to ~Wb (and the other objections) put forward by the Motor Groups. The Motor Groups were hardly simply conveying the reactions of a mass membership among ordinary motorists; but they did establish a highly visible rallying-point for mass opposition to *b*. The arguments they offered to stimulate this opposition may well have been judged to have more popular appeal, especially given their source, than the arguments that could be mustered in favor of *b*. With the representatives, recognized if to a large extent self-appointed, of the mass of motorists vociferously opposed to the proposal, the Ministry faced a case difficult to rebut effectively in popular terms; and for allies it had only a small group of academic thinkers, without any means of their own of mobilizing organized public support.

Let us rewrite the program once more, this time to represent the true relation between the Ministry's use of ~Wb and the vociferous opposition of all the Motor Groups. At the same time, the connection between action by the GLC and endorsement by the Ministry of Transport can be made more visible; the connection seems to be that neither will push on with a policy that the other opposes. The program, thus rewritten, would now run, after Phase A,

Is the policy S or E?
Is the policy K?
Is the policy W?
Is the policy J, i.e., a policy that arouses vociferous opposition, which cannot for the time being be dissipated, from concerned groups outside Whitehall?
Is the policy L, i.e., a policy that the GLC accepts without protest?

The rule for adoption will be

If Kx or ~Wx or Jx or ~Lx, reject the policy, i.e. (finally) ~Nx;
if ~Kx and Wx and ~Jx and Lx and (Sx or Ex) accept it, i.e. (finally) Nx.

The results of putting proposals *a*, *b*, *c*, and *d* through the program are:

Sa & ~Ea & ~Ka & Wa & ~Ja & La;
~Sb & Eb & ~Kb & Wb & Jb & (Lb v ~Lb);
~Sc & ~Ec & Kc & Wc & ~Jc & Lc;
~Sd & ~Ed & Kd & Wd & (Jd v ~Jd) & (Ld v ~Ld),

with *a* adopted by the rule, while *b*, *c*, and *d* are all rejected. (I have put p v ~p where the evidence I have does not warrant asserting one rather than the other.)

It might be asked, is not this last program just the program internal to the Ministry of Transport? What sense is there to ascribing it to the whole set of stations taken together? It is the Ministry, for example, that holds Wb in spite of the opposite contention from the Motor Groups; and the Ministry that rules out *b* on other grounds, namely, the fact of vociferous opposition from the Motor Groups rather than its content.

The program in this form may indeed be looked upon as a program employed by the Ministry of Transport; and this way of looking upon it corresponds to the paramount authority that the Ministry exercised on the issue as circumscribed in Phase A. But the operations of other stations by no means become superfluous. Those other stations had to operate for the Ministry of Transport to see, for example, just what are the most likely proposals in the field and what sort of support or opposition they engender. (Perhaps they need not have operated so publicly; on the other hand, the Ministry might have been interested in such points as seeing whether any spontaneous reactions in favor of *b* would arise when the Motor Groups published their objections; and the Ministry could not prevent them from being published anyway.) The schema and the earlier forms of program show that a program ascribed to the discussion need not be a program internal to the Ministry: the present program can equally well be looked upon as an internal program or as a program for the whole network, formulated from the Ministry's point of view.

6 Fuller programs; extra dimensions; further questions

The S-stable schema and each of the following programs, whether claiming S-stability or P-stability only, offer a sensible basis for predicting the fate of proposals like *a* or *a′*, *b*, *c*, and *d* in further rounds of discussion. The conjecture, which one might have formulated at the end of the first round, that the second round would be like the first in the respects manifested by one or another of these representations, was so far borne out that at the least the first signs of a regularity could be discerned; and these first signs give some credit to the hypothesis that further rounds will run much the same course.

Of course, the scope of such a hypothesis is narrow, embracing only four proposals or kinds of proposals. But this narrowness is in part the effect of the drastic simplifications used in the present book to keep the exposition within bounds. The programs given could be readily enlarged to cover the most prominent proposals left out, by adding to the considerations invoked by the Ministry of Transport and the GLC a concern for amenities similar to Buchanan's Ax, though appreciably less sensitive to the damage done by traffic. It was chiefly for this reason that proposals regarding monorails and overhead road-networks for tiny commuters' cars were rejected during the period surveyed;[1] and one might predict it will be for this reason that the proposal for automatic taxis will be turned down, too. All such proposals require the intrusion of massive works into central London streets.

The next stage in expanding any of these programs might well be to extend them to cover, besides proposals directly bearing upon traffic congestion, proposals that affected or that might have affected the fate of these even though they bore directly upon other matters. The prime instance of such a proposal is one, advanced several times by the Motor Groups, for an independent roads authority or roads board that would raise funds for road-construction and carry out all major projects, presumably on a larger scale than the Ministry of Transport contemplated doing.[2] If the Ministry of Transport had wished to, it could have sought a bargain in which this proposal was accepted on condition that the chief method used by the roads authority for raising funds would be road-pricing. Just such a proposal, combining a roads authority with road-pricing related not only to the optimum level of road-use but as well to the optimum level of investment in roads, was in fact advanced by a leading member of the Economists' Group during the period.[3]

Confidence in its own merits as well as respect for the principle of Treasury control may have led the Ministry to oppose any suggestion of an independent roads authority. But the idea of raising funds for roads chiefly or exclusively by road-pricing could be detached from the proposal; and on this point the Ministry of Transport might have sought a compromise with the Motor Groups which would have left its powers intact. It is a very remarkable fact that (so far as I have been able to discover) not the slightest tendency toward such a compromise appeared in the operations of the Ministry of Transport, in spite of some fairly obvious hints from the Motor Groups that their objections could be silenced by an assurance from the Government that if road-pricing (the 'congestion tax' as it was called, no doubt somewhat to its injury) were brought in, other taxes on motorists would be reduced to compensate.[4] Officials at the Ministry could have anticipated Treasury resistance to giving up those other revenues; but why did they not make a determined effort at Cabinet level to overcome the resistance? The answer, which would be represented in a yet more comprehensive program by reasons having this effect, seems to be that road-pricing did not offer enough in the way of extra political advantages, *vis-à-vis* increased parking controls, to be worth the effort in the eyes of the Ministry. Its visible effect in checking congestion would not be so much greater as to attract substantial differential political support. Its effect in selecting road-users—attracting onto the roads users with more economic (monetary) reason for being there, driving off those with less—would not translate into greater political support; it might do the reverse, since those who were driven off might be very disgruntled. I expect, in fact, that the only chance road-pricing has of being adopted depends on parking controls becoming too complicated and cumbersome to enforce, for example, through requiring control of existing privately owned parking space. Possibly if the costs it is to cover were to include damage to amenities, road-pricing might be brought in when and if it becomes politically more urgent to protect amenities than it is now. But in spite of the clamor about the Buchanan Report, very little political force has gathered behind his sensitive amenity reason Ax.

7 Significance of the illustrative programs: virtues of the issue-machine approach

The sketch just given of one program nesting within a larger one that in its turn gains light from nesting within one yet more comprehensive corresponds to readily accepted notions about moving for further explanation from histories narrower in scope to histories broader. Questions that can hardly be formulated within a given scope can be laid out for inspection if the scope is expanded. The attraction of the issue-machine idea thus depends in part on the way that it runs close to familiar notions about historical investigation—not only in conception, but also in practice. The case-history recounted in this paper is not after all so very different, when the symbolism has been allowed for, from many case-histories of a familiar sort, written simply to meet intuitive standards of relevance.

Even so, with the aid of the symbolism and with the issue-machine idea as a stimulus, the present case-history does make the departures predicted from ordinary practice. Personalities are thrust out of account (with a regrettable loss of color); even groups are given subordinate treatment, both as regards the struggle for power internal to them and their struggle with each other. Instead, the issue itself and the arguments about it assume special prominence. I am not suggesting that all case-histories should be written this way; I am contending that this way, among others, has its uses.

Some of the major uses can be gathered from the present case-history, in spite of its imperfections. The schema and the various programs of reasons each have at least a plausible footing; and taken together they add up, I think, to a tolerably accurate history. I have had to simplify so drastically for expository purposes that none of them appears with the distinctions drawn and the details given which would give them an entirely solid footing. Yet they suffice for my main purpose; they suffice as an illustrative basis for formulating the sorts of questions that the issue-machine idea raises, and in raising promises to be useful.

These questions include: On what subjects do what political systems have issue-processing programs that are stable for several consecutive rounds? The present illustration shows that this question is likely to have a different answer from the question,

What subjects are wholly matters of internal processing for one or another formal organization belonging to the system? Having identified the subjects, one would want to know of any one program, Is it P-stable only? Or is it S-stable as well? If it is S-stable, various forms have to be allowed for as possibly significantly different politically: discrete rounds or overlapping ones (as in the S-stable schema given here); networks admitting of repeated interventions by any station or networks assigning each station a fixed place in the sequence; networks simple or branching. P-stability itself may be manifested in various forms: in longer and more elaborate programs than any given here; in programs that give explicit room for meliorative reasoning as well as peremptory; in programs that end up, not simply with adoption or rejection, but with a range of outcomes indicating the probability of future adoption. (Even if one is skeptical about the chances of road-pricing ever being adopted, it would make good sense to distinguish its fate in 1968 from being rejected out of hand; it was still a live option.)

Answers to these questions would provide a mass of data for comparison and causal analysis; a mass, moreover, sufficiently formalized, one might hope, to facilitate comparison and analysis far beyond what can be attempted with the mass thrown up by familiar, intuitively-written case-histories. In particular, one might hope to identify, in the very form of the relevant programs, the biases of political systems and the factors that keep the biases in force. Just what reasons in what positions in relevant programs bias the British political system, for example, against giving more weight to long-run considerations of amenities in city life? And what sorts of changes in institutions as well as in the distribution of opinions (among voters and otherwise) would have to occur for the bias to diminish?

It should be clear that the issue-machine approach produces reasonable candidates for the title of scientific explanation. Indeed, if the P-stable program with or without scoring can be truly ascribed to the decision-making process in the United Kingdom bearing upon traffic congestion, then given further proposals and calculation of the bearing upon them of individual considerations, the program could produce genuine (temporally prior) predictions about the fate of these proposals. It is true that success would not establish the truth of ascribing the program beyond question: Success might be brought about even if the program was never true of the process, or had ceased to be true before the event predicted; for compensating changes might have occurred in the real, undetected program. But this possibility is common to all empirical hypotheses.

The effect of ascribing the program can be summed up by a scheme of explanation fully exemplifying Popper's and Hempel's classical outline: (L, the lawlike premiss) 'If such and such conditions are fulfilled—namely, the combination of tests expressed in the program, then proposals of such-and-such characteristics will be adopted or rejected (and with such-and-such relative scores)'; but (C, the condition-premiss) 'By the ascription of the program, such-and-such conditions are fulfilled.' Therefore, (E, the explanandum), 'Proposals of such-and-such sorts will be adopted or rejected (and with such-and-such relative scores).' Moreover, there is a substantial approximation to generality as well as universality in the form of lawlike premiss in this instance; for the lawlike premiss asserts in effect that a certain exact function holds (for phenomena in the United Kingdom)—the program taking the place and doing the duty of an equation. The result of calculation in either case is of course logically (or mathematically) necessary; but whether or not the calculation is the suitable one to perform is a contingent (empirical) matter.

One virtue of the issue-machine approach, which I might ascribe to it in closing, is perhaps almost wholly methodological or philosophical. Perhaps to someone more experienced in empirical research than I it will already be familiar, and not a virtue in any way distinctively ascribable to the approach. But to me at any rate it is a remarkable virtue of the issue-machine approach that it makes plain to anyone working upon it how artificial in construction the program is—without disqualifying it as a useful device for approaching the true description of the real process in view. One aims the first crude construction in the direction of the process and then refines the construction until it is a device capable of passing certain tests as to explanation and prediction. Other forms of description (historical narration, for example) may involve artifices of the same dimensions if not of the same sort; but mask them so that they do not call for systematic correction. It is an advantage, perhaps in more ways than teaching a philosophical lesson, to have the artifices explicit and palpable—disturbing enough to compel correction and hence advances in description.

Notes

1. Aims of the present study: chiefly, to illustrate the issue-machine approach

1 See David Easton, *The Political System* (New York: Knopf, 1953; 2nd ed., 1971); and Karl W. Deutsch, *The Nerves of Government* (New York: The Free Press, 1963).

2 See, for example, James G. March and Herbert A. Simon, *Organizations* (New York: Wiley, 1958), especially pp. 141–8, 177–80 and 212; and G. P. E. Clarkson, *Portfolio Selection: A Simulation of Trust Investment* (Englewood Cliffs, N.J.: Prentice-Hall, 1962). Directly inspired by Simon's fundamental work on simulating human thought patterns, Clarkson's work answers only in part to Simon's and March's proposals about research on formal organizations, since it simulates, not a collective program for issue-processing in which a number of persons are active, but the program used by one bank officer in making investment decisions. Otto A. Davis and Frederick H. Rueter study a collective program in their paper 'A Simulation of Municipal Zoning Decisions', *Management Science*, 19 (1972), pp. P-39–P-77. Their approach, in general conception and in some details, turns out to be much like mine, though we have worked quite independently. They focus on a shorter period (six months) than I and a less diverse and numerous set of participating 'stations' (all parts of the city government of Pittsburgh); and they practised continuous observation, to a degree that was not feasible for me, or generally feasible, of the decision process which they studied. One aspect of my aims in this book is to see whether comparable results regarding an issue-processing program—less precise, but still comparably useful—can be obtained when continuous observation (e.g. sitting in at all the relevant meetings, or even a sample) is not feasible.

2. Changes in the context of traffic policy discussion, 1963–8

1 *Parking—The Next Stage: A New Look by the Ministry of Transport at London's Parking Problem: July 1963* (London: HMSO, 1963).

2 Buchanan Report, *Traffic in Towns: A Study of the Long Term Problems of Traffic in Urban Areas* (Reports of the Steering Group and Working Group appointed by the Minister of Transport) (London: HMSO, 1963).

3 M. K. D. Goldrick, 'The Administration of Transportation in Greater London' (unpublished Ph.D. thesis, University of London, 1967), pp. 220–5; cf. GLC Minutes 1965, pp. 347–53.

4 Goldrick, *op. cit.*, pp. 226–7; *cf.* GLC Minutes for 19 November 1968, pp. 627–8.

5 See, for example, as very late evidence of this harmony, the approving comment by Alderman Ted Castle, the chief opposition speaker on traffic policy, regarding the defence of Robert Vigars, Tory chairman of the GLC Highway and Traffic Committee, of traffic management as having useful results, GLC Minutes for 30 January 1968, p. 13.

6 Goldrick, *op. cit.*, p. 262.
7 Cmnd. 3686.
8 See GLC Minutes for 19 December 1967, p. 751.
9 See *A Parking Policy for London* (London: GLC, 1968).
10 The break became fully visible, perhaps, only in March 1969 and afterwards, see *e.g.* GLC Minutes for 25 March 1969, p. 190; but the line taken, *e.g.*, by Castle's questions in the preceding fall, and the division forced by Castle early in December (see GLC Minutes for 3 December 1968, p. 695), on having an eight-lane highway rather than a six-lane one, implied the break existed well before March.
11 *Cars for Cities: A Study of Trends in the Design of Vehicles with Particular Reference to their Use in Towns* (Reports of the Steering Group and Working Group appointed by the Minister of Transport) (London: HMSO, 1967).
12 See Report of Highways and Traffic Committee in GLC Minutes for 10 October 1967, p. 561.
13 Smeed Report, *Road Pricing: The Economic and Technical Possibilities* (Report of a Panel set up by the Ministry of Transport) (London: HMSO, 1964).
14 See *The Times*, 11 June 1964, p. 12.
15 Central Statistical Office, *Annual Abstract of Statistics*, No. 108 (London: HMSO, 1971), Table 240, p. 218.
16 *Better Use of Town Roads: The Report of a Study of the Means of Restraint of Traffic on Urban Roads* (London: HMSO for Ministry of Transport, 1967). See in particular Mrs Castle's foreword.

3. The full list of proposals; and an issue-machine sketch of their fate

1 Buchanan Report, *Traffic in Towns: A Study of the Long Term Problems of Traffic in Urban Areas* (London: HMSO, 1963), Report of the Steering Group, par. 29.
2 *Traffic in Towns*, p. 11.
3 *Ibid.*, p. 26.

4. Recourse to a simplified approach

1 Most conveniently as set forth in G. H. von Wright, *Norm and Action* (London: Routledge & Kegan Paul, 1963); see also, by the same author, *An Essay in Deontic Logic and the General Theory of Action* (Amsterdam: North-Holland, 1968).
2 I have in mind chiefly N. D. Belnap, Jr., *An Analysis of Questions: Preliminary Report* (Santa Monica: System Development Corp., 1963 [Technical Memorandum TM–1287]). See also David Harrah, *Communication: A Logical Model* (Cambridge, Mass.: MIT Press, 1963), especially Chapter VI.

5. Two themes of a simplified approach: S-stability versus P-stability

1 Speech of 22 August 1963, reported in *The Times* 23 August 1963, p. 6.
2 For full explanations, see the Smeed Report (*Road Pricing: The Economic and Technical Possibilities*); or G. J. Roth, *Paying for Roads: The Economics of Traffic Congestion* (Harmondsworth: Penguin, 1967).
3 E.g., Beesley himself; Christopher Foster; J. M. Thomson.
4 Buchanan Report, *Traffic in Towns: A Study of the Long Term Problems of Traffic in Urban Areas* (published 27 November 1963) reported in *The Times* 28 November 1963, p. 12.
5 In October 1963 he became professor at the Imperial College of Science and Technology.
6 The British Road Federation includes the following groups (among many others): Asphalt and Coated Macadam Association; Cement and Concrete Association; Federation of Manufacturers of Construction Equipment; Motor Agents Association; Road Haulage Association; Roller Owners Association; Society of Motor Manufacturers and Traders. *Cf.* BRF Bulletin No. 402 (August 1970), p. 120. There are also some 40 or 50 firms that belong to the Federation directly (personal communication from the Director, 11 September 1970).
7 Comment on Marples' remarks (at the time of the publication of *Parking—The Next Stage*) by the Standing Joint Committee of the Royal Automobile Club, the Automobile Association, and the Royal Scottish Automobile Club. *The Times* 9 July 1963, p. 6.
8 Speech at Birmingham 23 September 1963 by Lord Gosford, Chairman of the British Road Federation, reported in *The Times* 24 September 1963.
9 Comments by Wilfrid Andrews, Chairman of Road Campaigns Council, and by Standing Joint Committee of RAC, AA, and RSAC, reported in *The Times* 28 November 1963, p. 10.
10 The Minister (Marples) said, 'No one can yet say whether [road-pricing] is desirable.' Action on the Smeed Report had not been decided upon 'but I shall not funk it.' *The Times* 11 June 1964, p. 12.
11 Comments by RAC and BRF, *The Times* 11 June 1964, p. 12.
12 *Buchanan and After* (BRF, 1 July 1964). See also the report in *The Times* 2 July 1964, p. 9, of remarks by Lord Gosford, Chairman of the BRF.
13 Speech at Bristol 14 April 1965, reported in *The Times* 15 April 1965, p. 8.
14 Statement 10 December 1965, reported in *The Times* 11 December 1965, p. 12.
15 *The Times* 11 December 1965, p. 6.
16 GLC Minutes for 19 July 1966, p. 426.
17 Cmnd. 3057.
18 *The Times* 13 September 1966, p. 8; 19 September 1966, p. 9; 21 September 1966, p. 10.
19 10 October 1966, p. 9.
20 Reported in *The Times* 17 October 1966, p. 7.

21 *Ibid.*
22 Letter from A. C. Durie, Director General of the AA, in *The Times* 19 October 1966, p. 13.
23 Report of meeting and of reaffirmation at the meeting of opposition to road-pricing, in *The Times* 24 October 1966, p. 11.
24 *The Times* 4 November 1966, p. 12.
25 Cmnd. 3481.
26 *E.g.*, *The Times* leader 11 June 1964, p. 13, pronouncing road-pricing (a congestion tax) acceptable only in the context of a reform of the traffic taxation system, with the global sum of revenue kept at about its present level; Mrs Castle's statement at the opening 27 June 1967 of the new Road Research Laboratory denying that she had made up her mind in favor of road-pricing pending the resolution of 'technological problems'—see *The Times* 28 June 1967, p. 2; or a statement by the economist Roth deploring the delay in acting on the Smeed Report—see *The Times* 3 July 1967, p. 2.
27 In April 1966 the Institute published a report by G. J. Roth—*A Self-Financing Road System*, favoring road-pricing. See *The Times* 29 April 1966, p. 8. It had previously published a study of parking control by G. J. Roth: *Paying for Parking* (1965).
28 In *A Strategy of Decision* (New York: The Free Press, 1963), C. E. Lindblom and I portrayed peremptory reasoning as imposing constraints on meliorative reasoning (thus utilitarianism is saved from leading traditional objections). Here meliorative reasoning figures as a source of constraints imposed on peremptory reasoning; and accordingly one would expect systems or programs of peremptory reasoning to change only incrementally. Much remains to be discovered, however, about the points of focus for both sorts of reasoning and for incrementalism.

6. Fuller programs; extra dimensions; further questions

1 *Cf.* GLC Minutes for 4 July 1967, p. 410, with GLC Minutes for 10 October 1967, p. 561.
2 *Cf.* Statement by Lord Chesham for BRF, in *The Times* 4 November 1966, p. 12.
3 *I.e.*, by G. J. Roth, in *Paying for Roads: The Economics of Traffic Congestion* (Harmondsworth: Penguin, 1967).
4 See again Lord Chesham's statement, mentioned in note 2 (for Chapter 6) above; and *The Times* leader, 11 June 1964, p. 13, mentioned in note 26 (for Chapter 5).

Fold-out II

S-stable schema (n.b., not a program) for two rounds

First round

Phase A (*issue-circumscribing*) ? Nx_1 v Nx_2 v Nx_3 . . . v Nx_n ?

Phase B (*proposal-initiating*)
(1) (July 1963, Ministry of Transport) Sa , , , Na.
(2) (August 1963, Economists) Eb , , , Nb.
(3) (November 1963, Buchanan) Ac & Aa , , , Nc & Na.

Phase C (*interacting*)
(4) (July/September/November 1963, Motor Groups)
Ra & Ia , , , ~Na.
Bb & ~Wb , , , ~Nb.
Nc & Nd.
(5) (June 1964, Economists) Eb , , , Nb.
(6) (June 1964, Motor Groups) Bb , , , ~Nb.
Ac , , , Nc.
Nd.
(7) (April 1965, MOT) Kc & Kd , , , ~Nc & ~Nd.
(8) (December 1965, MOT) Na v Nb.
(9) (December 1965, Motor Groups) ~Na & ~Nb.

Phase D (*decision-taking*)
(10) (February 1966, Greater London Council) Sa , , , Na.
(11) (June/July 1966, GLC) Ib , , , ~Nb.
(12) (July 1966, MOT) ~Wb , , , ~Nb.
Na.

S-stable schema for two rounds (continued)

Second round

Phase A (*issue-circumscribing*) ? Nx_1 v Nx_2 v Nx_3 . . . v Nx_n ?

Phase B (*proposal-initiating*)
(1) (July 1966, MOT) Na′.
(2) (September 1966, Buchanan) Ac & Aa′ , , , Nc & Na′.
(3) (October 1966, Economists) Eb , , , Nb.

Phase C (*interacting*)
(4) (October 1966, Economists) Kc , , , ~Nc.
(5) (October 1966, MOT) Nb v Na′.
(6) (October/November 1966, Motor Groups) Bb , , , ~Nb.

Phase D (*decision-taking*)
(7) (July 1967, MOT) ~Wb , , , ~Nb.
Na′.
(8) (December 1967, MOT) Na′.
(9) (May 1968, GLC) Sa′ , , , Na′.

Fold-out III

Three programs illustrating P-stability

First program:
Questions ? Sx ?
? Kx ?
? Wx ?

Rule If Kx or ~Wx, reject the policy, i.e., finally ~Nx;
If ~Kx and Wx and Sx, accept it, i.e., finally Nx.

Results Sa & ~Ka & Wa , , , Na;
~Sb & ~Kb & ~Wb , , , ~Nb;
~Sc & Kc & Wc , , , ~Nc;
~Sd & Kd & Wd , , , ~Nd.

Second program:
Questions ? Sx v Ex ?
? Kx ?
? Wx ?

Rule If Kx or ~Wx, reject the policy, i.e., finally ~Nx;
if ~Kx and Wx and (Sx or Ex), accept it, i.e., finally Nx.

Third Program:
Questions ? Sx v Ex ?
? Kx ?
? Wx ?
? Jx ?
? Lx ?

Rule If Kx or ~Wx or Jx or ~Lx, reject the policy, i.e., finally ~Nx;
if ~Kx and Wx and ~Jx and Lx and (Sx or Ex), accept it, i.e., finally Nx.

Results Sa & ~Ea & ~Ka & Wa & ~Ja & La;
~Sb & Eb & ~Kb & Wb & Jb & (Lb v ~Lb);
~Sc & ~Ec & Kc & Wc & ~Jc & Lc;
~Sd & ~Ed & Kd & Wd & (Jd v ~Jd) & (Ld v ~Ld).

Index

73 14840